I THEREFORE POST HIM AS A COWARD

Further details of Poppyland Publishing titles can be found at
www.poppyland.co.uk
*where clicking on the 'Support and Resources' button
will lead to pages specially compiled to support this book*

Join us for more Norfolk and Suffolk stories and background at
www.facebook.com/poppylandpublishing

NORFOLK DOCUMENTS

Norfolk is fortunate in having a wealth of documents surviving from the past millennium. Many are cared for in the Norfolk Record Office at the Archive Centre in Norwich; others remain in private collections. Some documents (and audiovisual materials) are now available online; a few have been published in scholarly editions. However, there remain many fascinating papers known only to specialist researchers. The intent of this NORFOLK DOCUMENTS series is to bring some of these to a wider readership, taking advantage of recent short-run printing technology to present them at reasonable cost for anyone with an interest in East Anglian history.

Instead of being restricted to reproducing what the original author wrote, with all its puzzles of historical reference and sometimes of quirky handwriting, this series includes:

careful transcriptions of the documents;
introductions to set the originals in their historical context;
notes to clarify obscure allusions;
references to further reading;
pictures, either from the original documents or from other sources;
indexing of people, places and themes.

As with all Poppyland Publishing titles from the last few years, further resources and support materials are also being made available on the website **www.poppyland.co.uk**.

Also in the *Norfolk Documents* Series:

I Therefore Post Him as a Coward

An anatomy of a Norfolk scandal, 1836

by
Gill Blanchard

POPPYLAND
PUBLISHING

First published 2017 by Poppyland Publishing, Cromer, NR27 9AN
www.poppyland.co.uk

ISBN 978 1 909796 29 4

Designed and typeset in 10.5 on 13.5 pt Gilgamesh.
Printed by Lightning Source

Picture credits

Author: Cover picture, 17, 20, 65
Bristow, Mike 42 (both)
Heath-Caldwell Family Archive 10, 37 (Courtesy J.J. Heath-Caldwell)
Norfolk Record Office 7, (MC 404/1-3), 11 (MC 404/1-3), 34,35 (MC 1830/1, 852X7), 41 (DN/TA 368), 44, 45 (HMN 4/205), 51 (PD 170/4), 59 (LMA: ACC/1063/254), 60 PCC 1855. TNA: PROB 11/2205)

Content

Introduction

A public showdown in church between a knight and clergymen and a challenge to a duel over a woman of ill repute sounds like Victorian melodrama. Yet it happened in real life in July 1836. I came across this story several years ago when researching the histories of some houses in Burnham Westgate and nearby. The confrontation is laid out in a series of handbills deposited in the Norfolk Record Office. I became fascinated by why these people had resorted to airing their dispute so publicly and what lay behind it. The whys and wherefores of this event in Burnham Westgate in Norfolk form the heart of this book. It is a story that sheds a light on the social mores and class divisions of its time and place.

My thanks go to Anne Bailey of Burnham Market whose house history was central to this quest. Also to Jane Ridley who first pointed me towards the online transcripts of the reminiscences of Elizabeth Jones 1801-1866. These provided invaluable insights about the people involved. Her descendant, J J Heath-Caldwell who hosts these and much more on his website has been remarkably generous with his time and in allowing me access to the originals.

This book developed out of a short piece I wrote for my MA in Biography and Creative Non Fiction at UEA, so my appreciation goes to my fellow students and lecturers for their invaluable feedback. My own personal proof reading and feedback team must take credit for helping to transform my rough workings. Any mistakes that remain after their efforts are of course all mine. This book is therefore dedicated to Ian Buckingham and Robin Orton.

Gill Blanchard
February 2017

I

July 1836: A gross breach of decorum

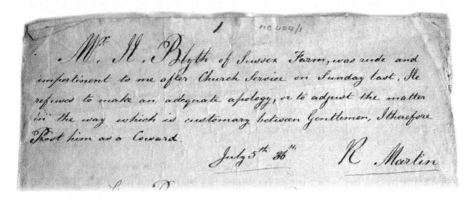

5th July 1836.

> '*Mr. H. Blyth of Sussex Farm was rude and impertinent to me after church service on Sunday last. He refuses to make an adequate apology, or to adjust the matter in the way which is customary between gentlemen, I therefore post him as a coward*'.[1]

With this provocative public challenge a scandal erupted in a north Norfolk village. A set of handbills fired off to local parishioners reveal how a woman of ill repute was paraded in church amid accusations of impropriety and a knight of the realm challenged a curate to a duel.[2] The church of St. Mary's at Burnham Westgate, just six miles from Holkham and nine miles from Fakenham, was the centre of this unlikely encounter between some of the most prominent figures in the local community.

The protagonists were Sir Roger Martin, a judge and prosperous farmer; Henry Etheridge Blyth, the curate and a well-to-do landowner; and Reverend Bernard Gilpin, the rector and a renowned theologian. All three men were parish officials, related to or on dining terms with the most influential families in the county and beyond, including the Nelson, Coke, Walpole, Townshend, Gurney and Pitt dynasties.[3]

At just before eleven o'clock on the morning of Sunday the 4th July 1836, Sir Roger Martin set out with his close companion and housekeeper Mary Ann Clarke. Together they made their way to St Mary's church from their home at Burnham Westgate Hall on the other side of the churchyard wall. Their route took them down the long driveway, through the double gates next to the *Pitt Arms*, then onto the edge of the market place. From here it took just a few steps to the right to reach the corner of the main road that leads to Docking.

Facing the rectory — the house where Sir Roger spent his childhood — they turned sharply to the right again to move alongside the long, low flint studded wall encircling the main portion of the churchyard. As the couple made their way along the narrow path towards the church's medieval wooden doorway it is tempting to imagine that they were observed by those stood outside chatting to friends and neighbours.

Entering the church they could see the grand memorials to Sir Roger's parents and maternal grandparents, laid into the floor on the left, next to the porch. As they continued up the central aisle towards the front of the church Sir Roger Martin and Mary Ann Clarke passed the poorest villagers who always sat or stood at the back. The small farmers, schoolmistresses, butchers, shopkeepers, publicans and other respectable tradesmen and women occupied the seats in the middle of the church. They may have just had enough time to gawp in enjoyment at the spectacle or avert their eyes in embarrassment as Sir Roger and Mary Ann drew adjacent. Even in spiritual matters, people knew their place in the early nineteenth century. Their place in church reflected their social standing: a physical embodiment of a class based hierarchy still seen by most people as ordained by God.

Perhaps there was a pause for a few seconds when the couple reached the front row. Then, in a 'gross breach of decorum'[4] Sir Roger Martin settled Mary Ann Clarke into the Martin family pew directly in front of the altar. The curate about to lead the Sunday morning service was outraged at her being publicly introduced into society in such a manner. For this 'woman of very questionable character for respectability'[5] had just been 'exalted to a place of honour that should only be occupied by a wife'.[6]

The man standing in the pulpit inside St. Mary's Church that summer's day was Henry Etheridge Blyth, who later described the sequence of events that unfolded.[7] He felt compelled to perform his duty and address Sir Roger out of regard for the respectability of his neighbours.[8] As the congregation began leaving the church at the end of the service Sir Roger remained seated. The curate took this opportunity to ask him to 'refrain from appearing so again: Sir Roger immediately took offence and abruptly left the church to join the crowd'.[9]

At five o'clock that evening his nephew, Bulkeley Glasse, visited Henry Blyth at home. Sir Roger Martin charged the curate with abusing him to his face 'from the pulpit in coarse and violent language'.[10] Bulkeley Glasse was there to demand an apology on his behalf or a 'hostile meeting to adjust the matter in the way which is customary between gentlemen'.[11] Henry Blyth refused.

Then, through his own emissary, Henry Blyth 'admitted that he was wrong in speaking to Sir Roger in the church'.[12] But, he asserted, the first affront had been given to himself and the ladies with him'.[13] Moreover, it was 'a feeling general in the congregation'.[14] The curate therefore refused to retract what he had said. Sir Roger's messenger returned once more with the same challenge – apology or hostile meeting. Once more Henry Blyth refused.[15] Just over twenty-four hours later Sir Roger Martin sent out a handbill addressed to the villagers denouncing the curate for his actions and 'posting' him as a coward for refusing to make amends or settle matters in a time honoured manner.[16]

Henry Blyth now felt it necessary to place 'his character in the hands of his friends' and responded in kind.[17] At this point Reverend Bernard Gilpin stepped in, presumably in an attempt to defuse the situation. A series of private letters passed between him and Sir Roger in which they reproached each other. The rector became frustrated by Sir Roger's intransigence and inflamed the situation further by having copies of their correspondence made into a handbill and addressing it to the parishioners.

It is hard to imagine how the churchman thought such a humiliating rebuke would resolve matters or encourage Sir Roger to behave differently in future. The knight found it equally as offensive as being berated by Henry Blyth. Unsurprisingly, Sir Roger countered in kind by also writing publicly to the inhabitants of Burnham Westgate the next day. 'I am', he said, 'averse to parading my opinions'.[18] However, given Mr. Gilpin's public reproach via the unusual form of a printed handbill 'it is the only course left me to pursue'.[19] Two more public responses were subsequently made in which both men justified their actions and refused to back down. By the time they were finished somebody had neatly copied all the claims and counter claims into one large document.[20]

Central to Reverend Gilpin's defence of his curate was his conviction that the baronet had an obligation to consider his social position and responsibilities. Wishing only for his 'truest happiness', the rector implored Sir Roger to set a good example to the lower orders.[21] 'To err is the stamp of frail mortality', he said. But 'to repair our error bears the impress of an ingenious mind'.[22] Bernard Gilpin went on to say he had no right to remonstrate upon Sir Roger's conduct, 'except when remonstrance becomes a duty I dare no compromise'.[23]

In his vigorous written defence of the curate, Reverend Bernard Gilpin accused Roger Martin of committing a gross affront to the propriety of the House of

A sketch of Burnham Westgate Church in the 1830s by Elizabeth Jones

God. He went on to lament Roger's ungentlemanly manner and 'violation of all decency'.[24] To finish off Bernard Gilpin said his wish was that Sir Roger's baleful example would not 'infringe upon the moral rectitude so essential to the good order and happiness of society'.[25]

Appealing to him as 'the most influential person in the parish',[26] Bernard Gilpin was particularly eloquent on the need for Sir Roger to set a moral example to society at large. In pointed comments on the family pew as 'a situation reserved by decency and propriety for the pride and ornament of domestic life' Gilpin implied Martin was denigrating the status and position of all wives.[27]

The family pew represented more than just a place to sit in church. Rather, it symbolised and reinforced social hierarchies and personal morality. The front two or three rows of seating were reserved for those ladies and gentlemen whose social position, education and wealth granted them a prime place. Many were passed down through generations. Seating that was privately owned belonged predominantly to the upper classes. These were often enclosed in lockable pew boxes and designed to offer the best view of services as well as make the occupants more visible to the rest of the congregation.[28]

Handbills were the social media of their time. By addressing his parishioners directly in writing Reverend Gilpin obviously wished to make matters public. So

To The Parishioners of Burnham

I am averse to parading my opinions before you, and should not ever have published this paper. but having been publicly reproached by Mr Gilpin in the unusual form of a printed hand-bill – and having been abused to my face from the pulpit in coarse and violent language by his Curate – it is the only course left me to pursue. If I have committed sin, that is between God and myself – no man has a right publicly to condemn me.

I have, I admit, offended against the rules of society established in this country, and have in consequence experienced the loss of female society in my house, even that of my nearest relations. I was aware that I subjected myself to this grievance, and to the rudeness of the vulgar: but while I admit this – while I submit to the usual penalties imposed by society – I will not allow the indecent violence of a party to prevent me from occupying my seat in Church as I may think fit, or from appearing in any other place where it is proper I should be present.

Except in the one circumstance above alluded to, my conduct has been I trust irreproachable, and my friend and companion whom Mr Gilpin is pleased to disparage, is I am convinced as kind, as generous, and as truly virtuous, as any member of his own family. In charity, I have not been behind my neighbours, but the exercise of that charity, which in its details is more frequently administered by a female, has been much impeded by unnecessary rudeness to Mrs Clark while in the performance of her duty in that respect.

I think it full time to put a stop to this state of things, so far as it is in my power, and therefore publish this statement for the information of those amongst whom Mr Gilpin's address of the 15th inst. has been circulated.

July 20th 36   R. Martin

Page three of the handbills circulated in 1836

too did Sir Roger Martin as they engaged in a paper duel. One can almost imagine copies being handed out at the church porch by a titled gentleman on one side and the vicar and his curate on the other, or possibly delivered by messengers from door to door.

Handbills, broadsheets, pamphlets and circulars had been a cheap, easy and widely used means of mounting an argument or exploring an issue since the early 1600s. They were used by all manner of people and organisations to spread news; defame people's moral character; raise awareness of grievances; advertise goods, services and events; declaim new wonders and campaign for social, religious and political reform.

In an age of rigid class distinctions, no national system of education and despite the majority of people being illiterate or only semi-literate, handbills still had the potential to reach a very wide audience. They were traditionally sold in bookshops and stalls, displayed in public meeting places and passed between individuals and groups. Those who could read them out loud at market places; outside churches and chapels and inside inns and coffee houses.[29]

The public claims and counter claims about morality between these three men were unusual in an era when mistresses, illicit relationships and illegitimate children were often widely known about but hushed up in public.[30] The seven adjoining Burnham parishes had their share of other newsworthy events and scandals from bankruptcies to murder well before the conflict between Roger Martin, Henry Etheridge Blyth and Bernard Gilpin.

2

The rudeness of the vulgar

Sir Roger's association with Mary Ann Clarke was not a new scandal. It reportedly first came to light in 1831, five years before Sir Roger paraded her so publicly within the parish church.[31] A damning account appears in a biography of Horatia Nelson, the illegitimate daughter of Lord Admiral Horatio Nelson and Lady Hamilton.[32] But until Sir Roger literally displayed his housekeeper as if she were his wife in that most holy of places, their behaviour could remain half hidden or ignored. The curate's furious reaction merely reflected the commonly held view that an unmarried couple living together was a sin. This was equalled only in immorality by having an affair outside of marriage.[33] Men might have mistresses, irregular relationships and illegitimate children as long as social conventions were observed and the sanctity of church and marriage nominally respected.[34]

The most likely reason for the hostility to Mary Ann Clarke was the existence of their 'adopted' daughter Ellen Clarke.[35] She was ostensibly the child of Mary Ann's deceased brother, but was at least partly brought up by Roger Martin and referred to in his will as his ward.[36] Whatever Ellen's parentage the reaction to Roger Martin and Mary Ann Clarke in 1836 is in remarkable contrast to the warm acceptance offered to Admiral Nelson's illegitimate daughter when she made her home in Burnham Westgate with his sister's family in 1817. Among those who befriended her were Roger Martin's sisters.[37] How much this was to do with the Admiral's status as a national hero and the subterfuge over Horatia's parentage can only be guessed at.

Sir Roger's feelings on the subject are known only through these handbills. Nevertheless, it is hard to ignore the possibility that his accusation of cowardice against Henry Blyth was partially influenced by being confronted by someone below him on the social scale — not a 'real' gentleman perhaps.

Whilst Henry Blyth was an educated and well-to-do farmer he was not quite in the same class as the baronet.[38] Roger Martin was born in Burnham Westgate on the 2nd February 1778 into a family proud to trace its ancestry back to a baronetcy granted in 1667. The family pedigree carefully stored amongst estate papers lays claim to blood relationships to some of the most prosperous and influential families in the country, including the Dukes of Norfolk.[39]

Yet, despite not being titled, the Blyth family did have considerable standing in the Burnham parishes. Twenty years younger than Roger Martin, Henry Etheridge Blyth was born in Burnham Westgate in around 1798. He came from a long line of farmers and clergymen.[40] Henry Etheridge Blyth's father (another Henry Blyth) had become the lord of Burnham Deepdale Manor in the early 1800s. This came with the right to appoint the rector of the parish of Burnham Deepdale, which had been granted to one of Henry's brothers. The curate was living at Sussex Farm in 1836. This 'neat mansion of white brick',[41] with a malthouse, blacksmith's shop, and brick and lime kilns lay on the edge of Burnham Westgate. Its 1,200 acres partly adjoined lands belonging to Roger Martin.[42]

Reverend Bernard Gilpin's moral stance against Roger Martin in 1836 put him into direct conflict with one of the most influential men in the neighbourhood. Moreover, as lord of Burnham Westgate Manor, Sir Roger had a nominal role in approving his appointment as rector to the parish in 1832. Reverend Gilpin was born in Whitehaven in Cumberland in 1772. After graduating from Christ's College in Cambridge he rapidly progressed up the church hierarchy, becoming a senior Greek lecturer and fellow at the university. He became well known after publishing his own poems as well as a joint work with W. H. Valpy of select theological extracts entitled *Anthologia Sacra*.[43]

'I was aware that I subjected myself to this grievance and the rudeness of the vulgar'[44] wrote Roger Martin to the parishioners of Burnham Westgate in the final handbill. He must also have been aware of the potentially devastating consequences on a gentleman's career, fortune and social standing of being the subject of such gossip or having an immoral relationship exposed in broadsheets and newspapers. It would be another twenty-eight years before a divorce could be granted without a private Act of Parliament. Even a legal separation was difficult to establish, illegitimate children were stigmatised and extra marital affairs brought public condemnation on those involved when exposed.

The sordid and dramatic saga involving the home secretary Lord Melbourne, Caroline Norton and her separation from her husband that had begun playing out in the press and courts in 1835 and 1836 could only have highlighted this awareness further. Caroline Norton had left her husband because of his violence. He accused her of having an affair with Lord Melbourne and sued him for seduction. Her husband lost the case, but Caroline's reputation was ruined and she was evicted from her home. As was the case for all married women Caroline had no rights over any money she earned or to custody of her children. Her husband prevented her from seeing them. Caroline's protracted public and legal protests led directly to the first child custody act in 1839 and influenced later legislation which granted some property rights to married women.[45]

It is not putting it too mildly to say that Sir Roger Martin's act in pitting himself against established social mores was subversive. It throws an interesting light on concepts of social class, duty and morality in a period of huge social upheaval, rapid industrialisation and agricultural depression. The French revolution was still within living memory and echoes of the seventeenth century English civil war reverberated amidst fears of revolt. Many feared that the monarchy could be overthrown once more. Norfolk was beset by outbreaks of machine breaking in the 1830s and across the country violent protests flared up regularly over major social and political changes such as the Poor Law Act of 1834 which ushered in a new system of union workhouses.

No wonder that Reverend Gilpin felt an 'imperative sense of duty'[46] to remind Sir Roger how vitally important it was for him to set a good moral example to the lower classes. Whilst acknowledging the 'bounds of his own station and age', Gilpin emphasised that social conventions were vital to the proper order and running of society. In response, Sir Roger admitted in the handbills that he had 'offended against the rules of society established in this country'.[47] As a result he had 'experienced the loss of female society in my house, even that of my nearest relations'.[48]

Roger was undoubtedly referring to two of his sisters, who all retained close ties to Burnham Westgate.[49] Whatever they thought of the situation and Mary Ann Clarke personally, respectable women were discouraged from mixing socially with women of a low reputation in case they were tainted morally.[50] Regardless, Sir Roger made it clear that he would continue to do as he wished as he wrote: 'If I have committed sin, that is between God and myself — no man has a right to publicly condemn me'.[51]

3

A hostile meeting

Roger Martin's demands for 'a hostile meeting to settle the matter in the customary manner',[52] and declaration that Blyth was a coward for refusing had the potential to turn this event from a local scandal into a national one. Duelling had been illegal in England since at least the medieval period – although often condoned.[53] This meant he could not explicitly call Henry Blyth out, although his language makes his intention clear.[54] Moreover, they both acknowledged the code of conduct associated with duelling through their actions. When Sir Roger sent his intermediary to demand an apology Henry Blyth responded in kind by arranging for a friend to communicate his responses.[55]

Whilst in 1836, the sight of duellists meeting at dawn, with pistols or swords had not completely vanished, growing disapproval and a perception of it as somehow un-English had driven it more or less underground. The last recorded duel between Englishmen took place in 1845 in Gosport in Hampshire, although one between two Frenchmen occurred nearly twenty years later in Old Windsor.[56]

As a young man of 26 in 1804, Roger Martin had been touched by personal experience. Family friend and neighbouring landowner Thomas Pitt, the 2nd Lord Camelford, died in March of that year aged 28 from injuries received in a duel fought at Kensington. Thomas Pitt was the second cousin of the Prime Minister, William Pitt the younger, and the first cousin of Admiral Sidney Smith. His father was the politician Thomas Pitt, the 1st Lord Camelford.[57]

The mother of the young Thomas Pitt was Lady Ann Camelford. She was the daughter of Pinckney Wilkinson, a rich London merchant and his wife Mary Thurlow, whose family had owned the large Cradle Hall estate in the Burnhams. Ann Wilkinson's dowry when she married Thomas Pitt included Burnham Westgate Hall, which her father had built. This would later become the home of Roger Martin and Mary Ann Clarke.[58] The Martins' family friend Elizabeth Jones (née Helsham) was later to wonder in her memoirs 'what possessed Mr. Wilkinson to build so handsome a house in so undesirable a spot I never could imagine'.[59]

Lady Camelford's daughter Anne Pitt married Lord William Wyndham Grenville in 1792. He was Foreign Secretary under William Pitt the Younger and later became Prime Minister, during which time he was responsible for steering the abolition of slavery bill through parliament. Elizabeth Jones went on to remark on how the marriages of mother Ann Wilkinson and her daughter Anne Pitt had been instrumental in the formation of an enduring friendship between the two families. Lady Ann Camelford and Roger's mother, Lady Everilda Martin, became the dearest of friends. Ann's daughter, Anne Pitt, was near in age to Roger's sister Anna Maria Martin, and the two women maintained a lifelong attachment and correspondence.[60]

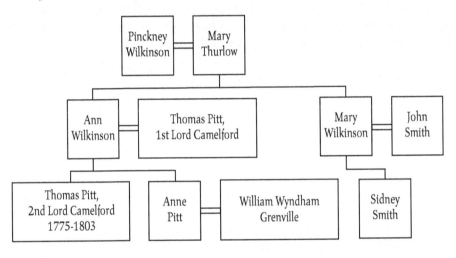

The Wilkinson and Pitt family tree

Thomas Pitt, the 2nd Lord Camelford, was just three years older than Roger Martin. Tall and handsome, his once promising naval career had been blighted by scandal. He was discharged from the Navy in disgrace after a number of incidents including insubordination and shooting a senior officer. Real stories of derring do — fights, imprisonment and spying — are mingled with almost mythical tales, including murder, from which the truth is hard to disentangle.[61]

The young Lord Camelford gained a reputation for being involved in duels, either directly or as a second to others. This was not something he even tried to hide as a letter to his sister Anne the year before his death makes clear. In it, he described how he had helped a comrade who'd fought in a fatal duel to get out of the way of the authorities.[62] His own deadly fight in 1804 reportedly occurred over disrespectful comments made by a comrade about Thomas Pitt's mistress. Meeting with pistols at dawn, he was mortally wounded when a bullet entered his chest. It took three days for him to die. Knowing the likely consequences for his opponent

Thomas Pitt readily admitted being the aggressor.[63]

Sir Roger Martin's social background and classical education valued chivalrous behaviour. Images of gentlemen fighting in defence of a lady's honour or to settle scores permeate literature and historical accounts.[64] Surely, when he issued his challenge to Henry Blyth in 1836 — thirty two years after the death of Thomas Pitt — Sir Roger saw parallels between himself and Lord Camelford in defending a woman against slurs on her reputation and himself against insults.

The tragedy of Thomas Pitt's death was of enough local importance to be noted on the flyleaf of one of the Burnham Westgate parish registers by the then vicar John Glasse. In yet another example of the interconnectedness of these families, John Glasse just happened to be both Roger's cousin and future brother-in-law.[65] The brief, but poignant note goes on to say how Lady Camelford had died the year before 'pining of grief at the career of her only son'.[66] This linking together of the two events leads to an obvious inference that the cleric felt it was a blessing she died before her son. In turn, Roger Martin's relationship with Mary Ann Clarke was to have an equally devastating impact on John Glasse and the rest of his wider family.[67]

4

The most influential person in the parish

To understand why and how the strange confrontation between the lord of the manor and clergymen took place in 1836 it is necessary to go back in time to untangle complicated family relationships, excavate other scandals, secrets and rumours and tease out local politics.

Roger Martin was one of eight children born to the 'kind and courtly'[68] Sir Mordaunt and Everilda Dorothea Martin (née Smith). Sir Mordaunt was born in 1740, and descended from an earlier Sir Mordaunt Martin of Long Melford in Suffolk, who was created a baronet in 1667. Sir Mordaunt became known as a 'soldier baron'.[69] During his long army career he served in the Royal Foresters as a Lieutenant and later became a marshal of the Vice-Admiralty Court in Jamaica. After leaving the army Sir Mordaunt took up farming in South Creake and the Burnhams in Norfolk.[70]

When Sir Mordaunt Martin and Everilda Dorothea Smith married at St. Mary's in Burnham Westgate on the 5th August 1765 the witnesses were Everilda's 'most intimate and beloved'[71] of friends, Ann Wilkinson and Ann's father Pinckney Wilkinson.[72] The new Lady Martin's ancestry is more obscure than her husband's. Her father, the Reverend William Smith, was ordained deacon in Lincoln in 1738 after attending King's College, Cambridge University. Although nothing further is known of his ancestry, published pedigrees state that he married Elizabeth Beaumont, daughter of Richard Beaumont of Whitby Hall in Yorkshire.[73]

The Smiths had arranged a marriage contract for their daughter Everilda before her marriage took place. The only details that survive are a reference to the contract in the deeds to properties in Stanstead in Suffolk. Sir Mordaunt also mentioned property jointured on his wife and her fortune in a letter and his will.[74] This meant that some, if not all, of Everilda's dowry or an inheritance from relatives was tied up in trust. This type of prenuptial agreement was common in an era when married women had few rights over their property unless it was protected by a marriage contract drawn up beforehand. They usually included a clause allowing a portion of the woman's inheritance or dowry to be retained for her own use. This would then pass directly to her children after her death, although her husband may have been allowed the interest or income from investments and rents.

Reverend William Smith and his wife Elizabeth moved to the Burnhams in 1742 following his appointment as rector in Burnham Ulph. Everilda Dorothea Smith was baptised by her father the following January. In February 1756 William bought

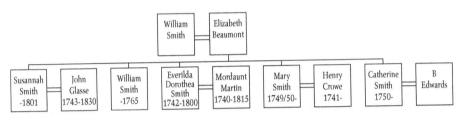

The Smith family tree

a house fronting the market place, which later became known as Burnham House.[75] The Martins benefitted from their family connections to wealthier branches in the highest tiers of the political and social scale. One of these was the Spencers. Surviving letters, bills and school records reveal that Lord and Lady Spencer paid towards Roger Martin's schooling and gave other practical and financial aid to the Martin siblings.[76] In a letter written by Lady Elizabeth Foster in 1793 Sir Mordaunt and Everilda's eldest daughter was described as a relative of Georgiana, the Duchess of Devonshire.[77] Georgiana Spencer was the eldest daughter of John Spencer, the 1st Earl, who was one of the richest men in England, and descended from the 1st Duke of Marlborough. After her marriage the Duchess became one of the most celebrated women of her time through her political activities and personal life, famously trading kisses for votes for the Whigs during an election.

The war hero Horatio Nelson, who was born in the adjacent parish of Burnham Thorpe in 1758, also referred to the Spencers as relatives of Roger Martin without specifying how.[78] Georgiana Spencer was in fact related distantly to Sir Mordaunt through her maternal line going back to John Mordaunt the 1st Earl of Peterborough. Confusingly, an obituary of Roger Martin refers to his mother as being the niece of the Earl of Peterborough, although it gets her first name wrong. Despite this claim no kinship between Everilda and the Spencer family has yet been established.[79]

One curious side note to Roger Martin's situation is that, whilst he was growing up his relative Georgiana, the Duchess of Devonshire, and Lady Elizabeth Foster were subject to a great deal of gossip and reproach, and at times ostracism, because of their own behaviour. Georgiana's husband had a long standing affair with Lady

Foster with all three living together in the same household for some time. Both women embarked on a number of relationships with well known figures and had children by the Duke and others. After Georgiana's death in 1806, Lady Foster married the Duke. Roger Martin's antics in 1836 seem mild in comparison.

Fleeting glimpses of the intermingled Martin and Glasse families are evoked in the reminiscences of Elizabeth Jones (née Helsham). She was born in 1801 and was related by marriage to the Martin family through her grandfather Henry Crowe, the rector of neighbouring Burnham Deepdale.[80] She was too young to know it first hand, but one tale that Elizabeth Jones heard was that Roger Martin's mother Everilda had sat for the artist Joshua Reynolds when she was still single and he had made an offer of marriage to her. One can only assume that Elizabeth Jones was unaware of the artist's reputation for painting courtesans and the intimate relationships he had with some of his models when she so happily recounted that particular story.[81]

The friendship between the Martins and Ann Pitt, Lady Camelford and her daughter Lady Anne Grenville was to be an important factor in the Martins lives and fortunes. Everilda and Ann were of a similar age and 'tenderest best friends',[82] although Sir Mordaunt undoubtedly knew the Wilkinsons and Pitts in his own right.

Letters from the Martins to both Lady Camelford and Lady Grenville survive from 1782 up to Lady Camelford's death in May 1803. They illuminate a relationship in which the Martin family looked to her for advice; shared confidences, joys and setbacks and obviously received all manner of assistance and financial support.[83]

Over and over again Sir Mordaunt and his daughters thanked Lady Camelford for her 'bountifulness'.[84] The first of these letters that survives, dated 18th May 1782, is typical. In it Sir Mordaunt paid his respectful compliments to her ladyship. Then he begged her to accept a flower he had seen her take notice of as a humble attempt to acknowledge 'his gratitude for her Ladyships essential kindness to his wife and family'.[85]

Reverend William Smith died in 1766, the year after his daughter Everilda's marriage.[86] Two years later Everilda's sister, Susanna Smith, married another clergyman, Reverend John Glasse of Pencombe in Hertfordshire. In keeping with tradition the wedding took place in her home parish with Ann and Pinckney Wilkinson as witnesses. John and Susanna Glasse retained strong ties to Norfolk, and the lives of their son, also named John, and his Martin cousins would become even more intertwined in the decades that followed.

After settling in Burnham Westgate the Martins immersed themselves in local affairs. Burnham Westgate, or Burnham Market as it was alternately called, is the largest of seven adjoined Burnham parishes. The other six are Burnham Deepdale, Burnham Norton, Burnham Overy, Burnham Sutton, Burnham Ulph and Burnham Thorpe. Today most of them are collectively grouped under the umbrella name of Burnham Market despite their separate identities.

Burnham Westgate was a prosperous market town in 1836 based primarily around agriculture and the wool trade. It lies on an ancient trade route to and from north Norfolk ports, principally King's Lynn, where goods and people passed to and from the continent and inland towns and villages. In Daniel Defoe's 1722 tour of Eastern England he wrote about corn being sent from the Burnhams to Holland through Weybourne, Cley, Masham [sic] and Wells-next-the-Sea. Defoe also had something to say on the other equally economically important but illicit trade operated by smugglers in the area.[87]

By the 1830s Burnham Westgate had a population of around 1,000 and 192 houses.[88] As in all small towns across Britain, the local Inn, manor house and church were at the centre of economic, political and spiritual affairs. The *Pitt Arms* — now known as the *Hoste Arms* — stands next the gates to the manor house where Roger Martin lived with Mary Ann Clarke. Here, in the parlour room at the back of the inn, he and his fellow local justices of the peace, clergymen, doctors and other public officials heard minor criminal cases, held coroners' inquests and dealt with other parish business.[89]

Sir Mordaunt Martin became renowned as an agricultural innovator working with famed agriculturalists such as Thomas William Coke of Holkham Hall to improve productivity through soil fertilisation.[90] They were part of the agricultural revolution which transformed farming practices from the mid-eighteenth century onwards and which had its seeds in north and north-west Norfolk.

Whilst Thomas William Coke rightly takes his place in history books for his crucial role in this process he was not alone. Sir Mordaunt helped develop measures to improve the growth of potatoes and other vegetables by introducing saintfoin into the country. Sainfoin, as it is spelt today, is a purple flowered drought resistant silage or hay crop that enriches the soil, and can be safely grazed by all farm animals.[91]

Mangel wurzels were first planted in England in 1788 and Sir Mordaunt soon began using the roots for feeding pigs during the winter. This practice became popular after he recommended it to Thomas Coke of Holkham Hall.[92] A 120 foot high Corinthian column paid for by public subscription was built at Holkham Hall in the mid-nineteenth century in honour of Coke. The carvings at the top of the monument feature turnips and mangel wurzel instead of the traditional Greek style acanthus leaves.[93]

Cultural life for Everilda and Mordaunt Martin in the Georgian era was characterised by exciting developments in the arts, literature and science with contributions from Dr Samuel Johnson, William Hogarth and George Frederic Handel, Henry Fielding, Mary Shelley, Jane Austen and others. Public buildings and houses were transformed through exciting architectural developments inspired by the likes of Robert Adam, John Nash, James Wyatt and John Soane. Romantic poets flourished and paintings by Thomas Gainsborough, J M W Turner, John Constable and Sir Joshua Reynolds became extremely popular.

A growing fascination with the natural sciences and exploration provided the impetus for exploration, experimentation and world changing discoveries. The British Museum was founded in 1753. The great naturalist and botanist Joseph Banks, who was born a year after Sir Mordaunt Martin, joined Captain Cook on his first great voyage to the South Pacific in 1768 at a time when Sir Mordaunt was beginning his own endeavours in soil improvement.

In 1775, the Martins employed Jane Arden as a governess. Jane was around sixteen or seventeen years old at the time. It was usual for young children to be taught at home. Whilst older children might attend a boarding school, girls who remained at home continued under the tutelage of a governess, whilst boys were given a male tutor.[94] The Martin girls would learn drawing, piano playing, reading, writing and arithmetic, dancing, penmanship and French.

Before joining the Martin household Jane Arden had been friends with Mary Wollstonecraft. Despite her young age, Jane is credited with being an important influence on the philosopher, writer and advocate of women's rights. They read books together and attended political and religious lectures given by Jane's father, John Arden.[95]

Although Jane Arden could have had little to do with forming Roger's character as he was only two when she left in 1780, it is possible to envisage her having a similar influence on the older Martin girls during the five years she was their governess. Anna Maria Martin was ten years old by this time. After she married Jane set up a boarding school in Beverley and published a number of educational works under her married name of Gardiner.

Although her social position as a governess was much lower than that of the Martin family, Jane Arden retained a lifelong affection for her old employers, even naming her daughter Everilda after Lady Martin.[96] On a return visit to Burnham Westgate in 1785 Jane wrote to her sister Ann of how happy she was to be back with them and the affection and delight with which her former pupils received her. 'I am in the very height of enjoyment in this charming family, their society is so refined, so intellectual!'[97]

Yet behind this public facade lay depression, marital problems, disagreeableness over tenancies, politics and money worries.[98] Throughout the 1780s, 1790s and early 1800s Sir Mordaunt wrote frequently to his benefactress Lady Camelford about his problems. Each time he acknowledged her financial generosity and good advice. Her 'bounty' to his family was mentioned over and over again. He frequently apologised for his own shortcomings, and on occasion sounded self pitying. In May 1782 for instance, he wrote of how he was ready to atone in any way she thought fit for his imprudence.[99] It is a mark of the depth of Sir Mordaunt's own bond with Lady Ann that he could share such intimate concerns with her.

There were lighter moments and good news in their lives. Sophia Elizabeth Martin took the time to describe a most agreeable ball she and her sister Everilda attended at Holkham Hall. The whole neighbourhood was there, she said. Around forty guests sat down to dinner and sixty to supper.[100] The company danced in the statue gallery and 'Mrs. Cokes dress was quite a fancy on a puce top with a crape [sic] train and white satin petticoat trimmed with gauze'.[101] There is a hint of relief in Sophia's words as she commented that there were almost as many men as women. They changed partners every two dances and 'Everilda danced the first two with a Mr Francis a relation of Mr Rolfes and I with Mr Coke'.[102]

The lives and later the loves and marriages of the Martins were of great interest to the Nelsons of Burnham Thorpe. Reverend Edmund Nelson and his son Horatio made a point on more than one occasion of noting how the young women were still single in letters to relatives.[103] In October 1792, Horatio Nelson wrote to his sister Catherine that Lord Spencer was visiting South Creake. Sir Mordaunt sent for Roger to show him to his relations and Horatio wished they would help the lad out.[104]

In October 1793, Sir Mordaunt conveyed his distress to Lady Camelford over how his ideas of true friendship had involved him in situations that broke his heart and left him an object of pity to all who knew him.[105] In December the same year he passed on details of his mortgages and plans to move house.

Both Sir Mordaunt and Everilda were depressed. He told Lady Ann how his feeling his life was a 'burthen to me may in some small degree account for her being in a similar state'.[106] Their marriage was obviously under strain on a more personal level. Sir Mordaunt went on to say: 'If I have failed in my endeavours to convince my wife of my sincere affection the day is past to expect success and I have nothing but misery to look to for the remainder of my life. But while I live I hope I shall ever wish to give her my proof of it which may be in my power.'[107]

Perhaps it was a coincidence, but the same month saw another act of kindness from their patron. Although Edmund Nelson at Burnham Thorpe claimed not to like to 'dwell in anecdotes of neighbours'[108] he felt compelled to pass on the good news to his daughter Catherine that Lady Camelford had settled upon Lady Martin for life £100 per year, over £5,000 in today's money.[109]

Lady Everilda was overcome by the kindness shown to her. Sir Mordaunt's letter of thanks for this gift extolling the virtues of Lady Camelford might well be considered overwrought and sycophantic to modern minds. It was impossible, he said, to think of her munificence 'without breathing ejaculations to providence'.[110] He wondered how his pen could 'do justice to what was in his heart in order to convince her Ladyship of his sincere and affectionate gratitude.[111]

Sir Mordaunt had another problem. Like many men of his social class he was involved in local politics and was nominated to become Sheriff of Norfolk in 1790.[112] In 1792 the Liberal party, or Whigs as they were commonly known, became bitterly divided over how the government should respond to the French Revolution. Now Sir Mordaunt found himself on the opposite side to Thomas William Coke of Holkham Hall and other companions and social equals. In 1793, the French declared war on England. The government advocated war against France which Coke opposed.[113]

Sir Mordaunt supported the position taken by Lady Camelford's husband Thomas Pitt and her son-in-law, William Wyndham Grenville. This was to favour fighting on the continent rather than at sea during the war. In addition, they supported various repressive Acts of Parliament in the 1790s which limited public gatherings, suspended Habeas Corpus, introduced a tax on printed works and forbade the formation of societies or groups for the purpose of political reform. Thomas Coke was against such measures.

Sir Mordaunt took what he felt to be a principled stance. If necessary for the good of the country he would even oppose his king. 'God forbid', he wrote to Lady Camelford on 6th January 1794, 'that I should ever be led by the hope of lucre to countenance conduct which I think has a tendency to throw this kingdom in the state of France'.[114] Sir Mordaunt became increasingly bitter over Thomas Coke's reaction and felt 'his present situation with respect to him was 'much misrepresented by many people'.[115]

Despite their growing political differences, he had — reluctantly — joined Coke's Corps of Volunteers as he had felt it his duty to pledge life and honour for whatever measures Coke thought most consistent with 'the spirit of the constitution'.[116] Nevertheless, he could not stay silent in the face of actions he felt opened the door to sedition. Time might yet convince others; Sir Mordaunt told Lady Camelford, 'that sincerity calls as loud upon a man to tell a rich friend of an error as a poor one'.[117]

One can almost hear the sniffy tone in which Sir Mordaunt then said: 'the conduct of indifferent persons is indifferent to me'[118] after telling her how greatly irritated he'd been by Thomas Coke's own expressed indifference to what Sir Mordaunt might say of him. He followed with a quote from Shenstone: "I will be no man's enemy but I can be half a friend'.[119] Then, 'if Mr Coke has a more sincere grateful friend than my self I shall envy whoever it may be whatever opportunity he may have of proving it'.[120]

Sir Mordaunt wrote many more letters of gratitude for Lady Camelford's generosity in the 1790s. At the same time as expounding on his political differences with Thomas Coke in 1794 he mentioned a reduction in his patrimony. Although

Lady Camelford had evidently complimented him on his carefulness, Sir Mordaunt reflected on how 'a man of business might have turned the seale the other way'.[121] He then pledged that no personal indulgence of his would injure his family as he was happy to adopt any plan of self denial she felt ultimately beneficial.[122]

At the same time plans were underway to overcome the obstacles which had prevented the marriage of Lord and Lady Martin's daughter Everilda. She was named after her mother and had been promised to the Reverend Thomas Barnard for four or five years, but the marriage had been delayed due to his low income. So in the latter part of 1793 Everilda and Lady Camelford enlisted the aid of Lady Elizabeth Foster.[123]

Lady Elizabeth Foster wrote to Lord Sheffield in September 1793 asking him to use his influence with the Lord Chancellor to bestow a good living on Thomas Barnard. She described Miss Martin as a 'very amiable girl'[124] who the clergyman was 'much attached to'.[125] But having only £100 a year meant 'their friends could not consent to the marriage'.[126] 'We are both therefore very anxious', said Lady Foster, that the poor young people should marry,'[127] before suggesting that the vacant living of 'Snoadlands or some such name' in Kent might be suitable.[128]

Success. Friends and neighbours celebrated the good news. Horatio Nelson's father Edmund wrote to one of his daughters from Burnham Thorpe in November 1793 to say 'we are looking every day for Everilda's marriage'.[129] It was he said, 'brought about by Lady Camelford's beneficence'.[130] The wedding went ahead in December 1793. When Everilda wrote again to Lady Camelford shortly afterwards she was still astonished 'at the fortunate change that has taken place in Mr Barnard's favour'.[131] Sadly, Everilda and Thomas Barnard were to enjoy only a few years together before his death in 1799.[132]

5

Free from every vicious propensity

Roger Martin had been sent to a boarding school in around 1791. The school was in the small village of Birlingham by the River Avon, around ten miles from Worcester.[133] It was run by Reverend Thomas Bradstock from his home and provided a classical education for up to six young gentlemen for a stipend of £50 a year.[134] Some or all of his fees were paid for by Lady Spencer, with contributions from Lady Camelford.[135] Perhaps this was the kind of result Horatio Nelson hoped for when Roger was shown off to the Spencers.[136]

Unfortunately, Roger showed a distinct lack of application, having more of a penchant for shooting than schooling. Edmund Nelson told his daughter in the winter of 1793 that Lady Spencer promised to provide for Roger. 'Yet the poor baronet is not easy in all points, what are honors or any advantages without care to use and manage them properly'.[137]

Detailed accounts for the period from Christmas 1794 to Midsummer 1795 were sent to his benefactresses. Roger's board and tuition cost £26 and 5 shillings. £1 and 1 shilling was needed to cover various bills to mercers, breeches makers and shoemakers and for washing and hair powder. In addition to which there was £7 and 3 shillings outstanding for pocket money advanced at different times.[138] By now Lord Spencer had explicitly expressed his purpose to Sir Mordaunt to provide for Roger.[139]

In August 1795 Roger's tutor tried to reassure Sir Mordaunt about his son's lack of literary attainments. 'His application and consequent improvement have been conspicuous, and I have no reason to apprehend an abatement of either',[140] wrote Reverend Bradstock. He confirmed that the Lady Spencer had consented to Roger continuing to shoot. 'It is', he said, 'certain that this indulgence has hitherto not only not retarded but hastened his improvement, because a greater portion of literary labour has always been stipulated and always performed on account of it'.[141]

At the same time Thomas Bradstock felt the necessity to point out the considerable expense involved in Roger's hobby. Although he only allowed him one pointer he did not expect the costs to be covered by the £33 a year allowance Roger had been given the previous year.[142] The schoolmaster assured Sir Mordaunt that he would not allow any sort of extravagance. Nevertheless, there would be 'some inconsiderable excess'.[143] He hoped Sir Mordaunt would not be reluctant to pay it 'as my young friend is wholly free from every vicious propensity and has no other amusement or expensive pursuit'.[144]

One senses that Thomas Bradstock was concerned he had overstepped a boundary. In a postscript, he sought to reassure Sir Mordaunt that he did not mean to overturn his judgment with regards to the amusement of shooting. As Lady Spencer had already given her consent he anticipated a refusal would be felt severely by Roger. 'Let me again repeat that I do not request this indulgence', he said; 'I only wish to make you perfect master of the circumstances of the case'.[145]

Sir Mordaunt refused. A couple of weeks later the schoolmaster pressed Sir Mordaunt further. He argued that 'in training young men it is sometimes impossible to do exactly as we could wish'.[146] Young men of Roger's age were, he went on, 'little disposed to hear the language of control'.[147] Reverend Bradstock did not wish to dictate what Sir Mordaunt's position should be, but felt that stern control and prohibition of an innocent amusement has 'been too often found to provoke vicious pursuits'.[148] He believed that Roger was willing to give up nearly anything asked of him 'without a murmur'[149] if it would gratify his friends. 'Shooting however is one of the few, perhaps the only, exception'.[150]

Thomas Bradstock finished by saying he only wished to do his duty and 'one part of that I apprehend to be the preservation of an affectionate and reciprocal attachment between a father and a son'.[151] Sir Mordaunt Martin did not take Thomas Bradstock's observations at all well. The schoolmaster had inadvertently struck a financial nerve and his response was equally emphatic:

> My son shall have his shooting licence and I will without a murmur relinquish the gratification of keeping a riding horse. He knows that the only one I now have is lent me by a friend and I will candidly tell you that having mortgaged the last here of my patrimony which is not in joynture to pay off my debts leaves me a balance of about £30 [ev]en Roger has commanded his portion of it. I hope neither you nor he will think that I drive him by "stern control" to "vicious pursuits". Permit me Sir to assure you that all I feel on this occasion does not prevent my being sensible of your kind intentions.[152]

There the matter rested for a couple of months. Unfortunately, the schoolmaster felt compelled to write to Sir Mordaunt again in November of that year, with much underlining of key concerns.[153] Despite his best efforts Roger's ideas of expense differed widely from those of the other students.[154]

I have laboured with much unremitting diligence both by arrangement
by authority to the confine his expences to his given bounds but finding
it impossible to succeed. I think it my duty to inform you that he has
already exceeded his allowance considerably and that under the existing
circumstances my present situation is extremely irksome I shall still restrain
him to the utmost of my power till the ensuing vacation when I must request
to you to relieve me from a responsibility so mortifying to my feelings.[155]

Passing copies of the letters on to Lady Camelford, Sir Mordaunt Martin wrote
to his son the next day:

For God's sake lose no time in clearing up to me the cause of so total an
alteration in Mr B's account of your conduct from the report he made you
at the last vacation. How to broach the subject to dear Lady Spencer I know
not. It certainly must be done but I will endeavour to avoid it till you may
enable me to indicate you or at least to plead your pardon by the best excuse
you can furnish me with and the best reasons you can give me to hope for
your rendering yourself worthy her future protection. Your poor mother did
not want such a check as this to prevent her recovering too fast. I wish you to
inform Mr Bradstock that my feelings at this moment are too acute to enable
me to answer his letter in such a manner as the importance of the subject
requires.[156]

Thus it was that in 1795 Roger Martin joined the East India Company. He was
17 years old when he was appointed to the Bengal branch on 26th March 1796. His
Writers' Petition — entry papers into the company's civil services — stated that he
was educated in writing and accounts, whilst the local vicar provided a reference
confirming the same. He was to spend the next thirty two years living away from
home.[157]

The East India Company was formed in 1600 to pursue trade in the region,
but ended up effectively ruling large areas of India, overseeing the beginnings of
the British Empire there. Company rule effectively began in 1757 and lasted until
1858, when the British Crown assumed direct control in the form of the new Raj.
By this time the company had become more of an administrative body than a
trading concern. Despite a lack of legal training Roger became assistant magistrate
at Burdwan in Bengal within two years of arriving in India. He was an employee
rather than an instrument of government. He subsequently became a magistrate
in Gorakhpur before spending several years as senior judge of the Court of Appeal
of Moorshedabad in Madras.[158]

6

The noble sentiments of his heart

Whilst Roger Martin began to build a career thousands of miles away on the Indian continent, his family's circumstances were changing too. By now his sisters Everilda and Louisa were married and his mother's health began to fail. It took months for letters to travel between India and England so he and his sister Caroline both kept journals to send to each other, like a newsletter.[159]

In 1798, Sir Mordaunt Martin led the local celebrations for Horatio Nelson's victory over the French at the Battle of the Nile and subsequently being created Baron Nelson of the Nile and Burnham Thorpe. A sheep was roasted whole and *Rule Britannia* sung by Mr Cater and the Burnham Ulph band. Sir Mordaunt gave a speech during which he recommended setting up a subscription for the families of those injured or killed.[160] As the crowd sang a hunting song which concluded with 'chuck in your half crowns'[161] he threw a guinea on the table to launch the fund. Altogether they raised three pounds nineteen shillings and six pence from those who followed suit.[162]

When Sir Mordaunt wrote to Reverend Edmund Nelson on the 11th October 1798 at Burnham Thorpe to congratulate him on Horatio's promotion he added that they had not heard from Roger recently. However, Roger had an appointment 'up the country'[163] which Lord Spencer had assured Sir Mordaunt was a mark of confidence.[164]

Roger was still only twenty-two years old when his sister Sophia indicated he was still being profligate in one of her letters to Lady Camelford. He had spent four guineas (around £135 today) to send a letter in April 1800 by overland conveyance having realised they had not received other letters from him.[165] Roger was very anxious to receive forgiveness for a previous letter he had written to Lady Spencer. Sadly, we do not know the contents, but he now 'felt himself quite a new man'.[166] He would not, Roger told Sophia, have used such an expensive means of sending it 'but that he wished by every possible means to convince us how much it was his resolution not to fall again into his old error'.[167]

Sophia Martin did not expand on what her brother meant when referring to his old error. She doubted if he had begun to save money. 'But', she went on to say, 'he expresses himself with great prudence on that head and says he has given up seeing company at his home upon finding his income inadequate to it, and that nothing unless it were to assist his father could induce him to run in debt'.[168]

Lady Everilda Martin's health began to deteriorate in the autumn of 1800. At first Dr Redfearn assured Sophia that her mother's complaint arose from extreme weakness and gave the strongest assurances of a perfect recovery.[169] He was mistaken. Soon afterwards Anna Maria and Sophia sent Lady Camelford the alarming news that their dear mother was in extreme danger.[170]

Lady Everilda Martin's death on the 21st September 1800 was met with an outpouring of grief from her children and closest friends.[171] Despite her own sorrow Sophia empathised with Lady Ann Camelford: 'You have lost perhaps the oldest, closest, certainly one of the sincerest and most affectionate of your friends and I feel for all that you must suffer'.[172]

It took months for the news of his mother's death to reach Roger Martin in India. By the time his reply was received in England nearly a year had passed. His sister Anna Maria forwarded his letter on to Lady Camelford and the Dowager Lady Spencer. 'The blow is a severe one for us all but the sad distance he is at must have greatly increased the force of it to him poor fellow, and it is grievous to us that we cannot be at hand to endeavour to soothe and comfort him'.[173]

In the meantime Roger had decided to help out his sister Everilda Barnard. She had been widowed in 1799 and had five young sons to bring up. Roger sent her a note for £50 which she received in April 1801, around the same time Roger heard of his mother's death.[174] Everilda Barnard could hardly contain her satisfaction at her brother's affection and generosity when she wrote to Lady Camelford about his noble character and selflessness. More importantly: 'how would my dearest mother have rejoiced and exulted could she have witnessed this'.[175]

Unfortunately, Roger had not managed to reform his old habits. Only a few weeks later Everilda was writing to Lady Camelford once again. This time she was 'grieved at the intimation you give me of my poor brother's turn for dissolution'.[176] As he was surrounded by so many who were prone to laxness and expense his sister felt it was necessary to urge Roger 'to habits of industry and clemency'.[177] However, she felt her own obligations to him given his recent kindness meant that any remonstrance from her would be met with ill grace. Instead, Everilda suggested that a hint from her Ladyship would have greater effect as Roger would be flattered by her great anxiety for his welfare.[178]

Another three months went by and Everilda had more news to pass on. Another letter had arrived from 'dear Roger',[179] who was offering to help her children. Everilda quoted what he'd written so Lady Camelford could read for herself 'the noble sentiments of his heart':[180]*They certainly ought not to be deprived of the very best education for want of money, and I trust before the most expensive time arises I shall be able to assist you essentially. I am sure I will do all I can, and I trust God will not keep any of your wants unknown to me. From the 1ˢᵗ of Jany 1800 I have deducted at the rate of £100 a year from my monthly salary, which I continue doing let what will happen during my stay in India this does not in the smallest degree inconvenience me.*[181]

Roger went on to say he particularly wanted to do something for his little godson Mordaunt Barnard, although he did ask if it would be better to treat all her sons alike.[182] Despite her joy Everilda did not feel she could take advantage of his generous heart by accepting deductions from his salary. Firstly, she could not forget the great expense their father had on his account. Then she wondered if Roger had acted on impulse and sufficiently considered how his own interests could be hurt by depriving himself of so considerable a yearly sum.[183]

The young widow's final point was that Roger was ignorant of the silent assistance she'd had from others quarters which answered all her present needs.[184] This was no doubt an allusion to another of Lady Camelford's gifts. Everilda resolved to 'wait a few years longer till he shall have established himself in the world and then my children shall glory in his help'.[185]

After their mother's death Anna Maria and Sophia Martin spent much of their time looking after various friends and relatives who were ill. By now their maternal aunt, Catherine Edwards, who was the widow of the rector of Hethersett, had suffered two strokes. Sophia accompanied her to Cromer to try sea water bathing in the hopes it would restore her shattered frame.[186] Their other maternal aunt Susannah Glasse died in 1801. Perhaps it was to take their minds off losing another family member or simply that they now had more time, but shortly after their aunt's death Sophia Martin set up a spinning school for poor women in the village and Anna Maria started a society for young women. Lady Grenville donated books and her mother Lady Camelford helped set up a money raising scheme involving the sale of donated beef and rice.[187]

Things were not going so well for Sir Mordaunt Martin. Around this time he feared he would lose the best part of the farm he had leased for thirty four years despite having improved it 'as carefully as if the land had been my own'.[188] He considered moving to Stanstead in Suffolk where he had a manor.[189] Fortunately, Sir Mordaunt's worries were eased to some extent by Lady Camelford's endeavours on his behalf and his remittance for his position at the Vice-Admiralty Court in Jamaica being put onto a sure footing for the future.[190]

In December 1801, Everilda Barnard 'received a most kind and understanding letter from dear Lady Grenville'.[191] It was his lordship's turn to nominate a boy for a scholarship at the Charterhouse school and that he would name one of hers if she wished it.[192]

The following year the Martin family celebrated Anna Maria's engagement to Reverend John Glasse.[193] Anna Maria felt unable to reject 'so much happiness as I trust will be served to me both here and hereafter by a connection with so truly exemplary a character'.[194] She did however hope that Lady Camelford would 'not think us imprudent to have engaged ourselves without an immediate prospect of settling'.[195] Anna Maria went on to say she felt her Uncle Glasse must be disappointed his son had chosen 'a being so thoroughly inferior to him as I am in every particular. Would I were perfection for his sake for no one is more deserving of it could it but be met with.[196]

There was more grief when the youngest Martin daughter Fanny (Frances) died only a few weeks after Anna Maria became engaged.[197] Anna drew great strength from the constant letters she received from her fiancé John Glasse. 'Every line of them proves the excellency of his heart, and that his mind is regulated by the purest principles of religion'.[198] She felt her own sad disposition of spirits had wounded him. Further, she hated being the cause of uneasiness to someone so beloved for whom she felt she was in no degree worthy. It was a consolation to both of them that Lady Camelford sanctioned their connection. Anna Maria wanted her to know how much it added to her happiness 'that what you so perfectly approve must have given satisfaction to my beloved parent who ever looked up to you as her tenderest best friend'.[199]

7

Erelong, all was sadness and sorrow

Roger Martin was still in India when the Martins' most generous benefactress Lady Ann Camelford died in 1803, aged 64. Her death was believed to have been caused by grief over the lifestyle of her son Thomas Pitt.[200] When he died the following year from the wounds he received in a duel there was little surprise among his contemporaries at his ignominious death. His sister Lady Anne Grenville inherited his share of their mother's estate. She and her husband then bought out the share that had gone to the descendants of her maternal aunt Mary Smith and sold the whole lot shortly afterwards. Sir Mordaunt Martin's fortunes were much improved by this time and he was able to buy Burnham Westgate Hall from them in 1805.

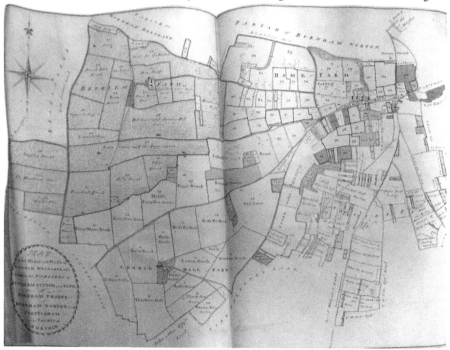

The estate survey and the hall

In the same year, Roger Martin's elder sister Anna Maria married their first cousin, the Reverend John Glasse at St. Mary's church in Burnham Westgate. Anna Maria was by now 34 years of age and John a couple of years younger. The ceremony was witnessed by her sisters Sophia Elizabeth and Caroline Martin. The Napoleonic war was still underway, with the Battle of Trafalgar fought and won

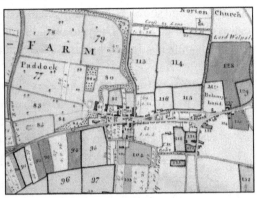

A detail from the estate survey

a few months later. Amid the celebrations the parishioners of the seven Burnham parishes mourned the death of Horatio Nelson. He was not just a national hero; he was one of their own.

Now most of his children were settled Sir Mordaunt Martin brought home a second wife after several years as a widower. Catherine was the widow of Edward North, lately the rector of Ringstead and daughter of another clergyman, Reverend Armine Syleham of Snettisham.[201] Their wedding in her home parish of Ringstead on the 4th August 1808 was conducted by Sir Mordaunt's son-in-law John Glasse. Elizabeth Jones recalled how the new Lady Martin 'brought with her two daughters, the one clever and severe, the other the exact opposite'. After their marriage, 'occasionally the Holkham carriage and four would drive up bringing Miss Coke and her stern governess, or Lady Anson and her sweet looking daughter'.[202]

In August 1811 Roger Martin was appointed as judge and magistrate of the district of Goruckpore. That same year his friends and family in England witnessed a brilliant comet.[203] Then, in 1812 Sir Mordaunt purchased the lordship of the manor of Burnham Westgate.[204] As well as being a knight of the realm he now held a position based on ancient rights dating back over a thousand years. With it came strong echoes of feudalism, fealty sworn to the Crown and obligations between the lord or lady and their tenants. Traditionally, those who lived within a manor received protection in return for certain duties. Although its function as a court of law for minor offences had been taken over by civil courts, the manor still controlled the leasing, buying and inheritance of copyhold land - a type of land tenure — until the copyhold system was abolished in 1922.

Small vignettes of life in Burnham Market in this period are conjured up in the reminiscences of Elizabeth Jones (née Helsham).[205] As well as being connected by marriage Elizabeth became very good friends with Anna Maria and her sister Everilda despite the large age gap, and her fondness for the Martin and Glasse families shines through in her anecdotes. There is a striking image of her seeing the 'blue feather and shoes'[206] that belonged to William Bulkeley Glasse in the hall when he was a small boy. It was he who would later act as his Uncle Roger's messenger over the dispute inside the church in 1836.[207] Elizabeth Jones recalled how:

> Every year we had one or more expeditions to the seashore where young and old were collected in the carrier's tilted wagon. My grandmother and Miss Martin the two timid ones, invariably sitting where they could watch the horse. This was always a day of freedom and wild enjoyment. Shoes and stockings might be taken off, and even my grandmother's slender ankles were visible.[208]

Again and again over the next few years came tidings of triumphs and setbacks in the war against France.[209] Everilda Barnard's eldest son Thomas died on board HMS Kite in June 1813 of wounds received in action against pirates.[210] Those in Norfolk experienced the terrible winter of 1813-14. 'Our sunny walks on the crisp snow were so exhilarating, and the sufferings and privations of our poor neighbours were so great'[211] wrote Elizabeth Jones in her memoir.

Elizabeth then recalled how the Allies entered Paris before the snow disappeared that winter. All the following summer 'was marked by rejoicing for peace. An ox roasted whole in the Market Place was a horrid sight, but the illuminations as seen from Castle Hill a very beautiful one'.[212] Her family visited Burnham Westgate 'and took part in festivals of every kind and degree, eating jelly off plates in Holkham Park, or humble plum pudding in the Market Place at Burnham, but always ending with a dance, one while in a meadow, and another in a malthouse'.[213]

Almost half a world away Roger was caught up in the Anglo-Nepalese War of 1814 to 1816, also known as the Gurkha War. This took place between the Kingdom of Nepal and the East India Company over border disputes and expansionism. Roger's surviving correspondence to his superiors, the Chairman of the East India Company and Lord Wellesley, the Governor of Burdwan, focused only on administrative affairs and the practicalities of fighting insurgents. The war ended in 1816 with the ceding of a third of Nepal's territory to the British.[214]

In Burnham Westgate news came of Napoleon escaping from Elba, armies mustering, and the 'glorious victory' at Waterloo in June 1815 along with reports of 'who had survived and who had fallen'.[215] Sir Mordaunt Martin died three months later, on the 25th September, aged 75.[216] Afterwards, his second wife, Lady Caroline Martin, moved back to Ringstead where she survived him for another ten years. Sir Roger inherited the baronetcy and Burnham Westgate Hall after his father's death, but did not return home.[217]

In England, victory over France was followed in 1816 by 'great commercial and agricultural distress'[218] Bad harvests triggered an agricultural depression that saw

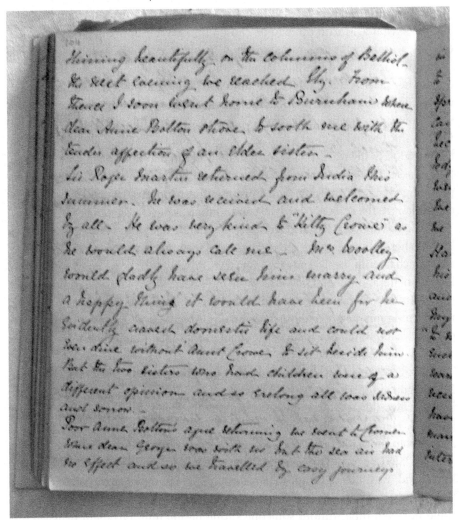

The return of Sir Roger Martin in the 'Reminiscences' of Elizabeth Jones.

food riots across Norfolk and elsewhere. Anna Maria Glasse, Elizabeth Jones and other local ladies ministered to the poor with nourishing soups as well as they could.[219]

That same year newspapers across East Anglia reported how 'Buxoo, a Bengalese native of Calcutta' was baptised at St. Mary's church in November. He had been brought to England by Captain Glasse, one of Roger Martin's relatives. This was probably a distant cousin by marriage as his Glasse nephews were still children. Buxoo had been taught the grounds of Christian faith and was baptised in the name of John Henry Martin. The ceremony was conducted by Roger Martin's brother-in-law Reverend John Glasse. The new convert was to return to India the following spring.[220] How and why Captain Glasse brought him to Burnham Market and the surname Martin came to be chosen for him must remain a mystery. One can only wonder if Sir Roger was somehow involved in the whole episode.

In 1816, the widowed Everilda Barnard, who had been living in Polsted House next door to her sister Anna Maria Glasse, moved to London to make a home for her son George Barnard who was a clerk at the Exchequer. Her other son William followed soon afterwards. The new neighbours of Anna Maria and John Glasse were Thomas Bolton, the brother-in-law of Horatio Nelson, and his family. The two families became closely involved and Thomas Bolton began acting as a churchwarden to John Glasse. This meant taking responsibility for maintaining the church property; providing what was needed for worship; presenting people who had offended against church laws to the archdeacon's court and administering church funds.

The following year, Horatio Nelson's illegitimate daughter Horatia was sent to live with her Bolton relatives, although she was seemingly unaware of her parentage until much later in life. Despite the official version being that she was adopted, the identity of her mother and father seems to have been widely known to others at the time.[221] In 1817, Elizabeth Jones and her mother Catherine Helsham took a house nearby and remained neighbours of John and Anna Maria Glasse for the next two or three years. When Elizabeth's sister died in 1818 their kind friends Miss Martin and Mrs Glasse were there to comfort them.[222]

Sir Roger Martin was appointed as second judge of the provincial courts of Moorshedabad in 1819.[223] Around this time he kept the promise he had made to his sister Everilda when she was widowed that he would do what he could to help her boys. Her fourth son William Barnard left the Navy after peace was declared and went to India where his uncle Roger could forward his interests.[224]

1828: 'Sir Roger Martin returned from India this summer'[225] wrote Elizabeth Jones, and 'was received and welcomed by all'.[226] He settled permanently at the hall. Elizabeth Jones felt that Sir Roger 'evidently craved domestic life'[227] as he could not even dine without someone sitting beside him. Elizabeth believed his sister Louisa would have gladly seen him marry. 'But, the two sisters with children were against it, so erelong, all was sadness and sorrow'.[228]

In fact there were three of Roger's sisters who had children – Everilda, Caroline and Anna Maria. There are strong clues that the main opposition came from Everilda and Anna Maria. Caroline had married Captain James Monro, a widower with eight young children in 1805. They had one son together whom they named Mordaunt Martin Monro. Caroline was considered a little eccentric by her friends in the village and rarely visited Burnham after her marriage.[229] Of the remaining sisters, Louisa had married a Captain Isaac Wolley of the Royal Navy in 1796, but had no children. Fanny had died years before and Sophia passed away in 1827; both without marrying.[230]

Anna Maria, and her husband Reverend John Glasse had two young sons. Everilda Dorothea had five sons from her marriage to Reverend Thomas Barnard; the second eldest of whom was named Mordaunt after his grandfather. When Everilda was widowed and left with five young sons to care for, she thought Roger noble for trying to assist her financially. Although more than thirty years had passed since then he obviously retained an interest in their lives.[231] As the only surviving son and bearer of the family name, such opposition by Roger's sisters is curious, unless they hoped that one of their own sons would inherit the estate. Roger was by now 50 years of age, so maybe it was reasonable to expect him to remain single for the rest of his life.

8

A harassed mind

Roger Martin's flaunting of his relationship with Mary Ann Clarke so publicly is connected to another scandal that occurred just five years previously, in 1831, involving his brother-in-law the Reverend John Glasse. The marriage of John Glasse to Roger's sister Anna Maria in 1805 linked the two families twice over as their mothers were sisters. Yet, despite coming from a wealthy background and his wife's substantial dowry, John Glasse was burdened by recurring financial difficulties.[232]

John Glasse was born in Pencombe in Herefordshire in 1772. His father – also called John – had previously been rector of Burnham Westgate. His mother was Susannah Smith, sister of Lady Everilda Martin and the previous incumbent's daughter. Educated at New College in Oxford, John Glasse junior was presented to the living of his father's old parish in Burnham Westgate in 1804. The Napoleonic Wars were still underway when he married his cousin Anna Maria Martin the following year.

For the first two or three years of their marriage John and Anna Maria made their home in one half of Burnham Westgate Hall, with the other half occupied by Henry Crowe, the rector of the neighbouring parish of Burnham Deepdale. Their two children William Bulkeley, commonly known as Bulkeley, and Mordaunt were born in 1806 and 1813.[233] Bulkeley was to always be an important figure in Roger Martin's life, including being his intermediary in 1836.

John Glasse came from a long line of clergymen, all educated at Oxford University. From the early 1700s each generation had at least one son who entered the church. They too had their share of tragedy. In 1809 came the ghastly news that his cousin Reverend George Henry Glasse had taken his own life over debts. However much was revealed publicly at the time it would have been difficult to avoid seeing the horrendous details rehashed dramatically across two pages in local newspapers two years later.[234]

Whilst expressing sympathy at his plight the *Norfolk Chronicle* spared none of the details of how George Glasse destroyed himself.[235] He was staying at a London

Inn whilst fleeing his creditors. In a tragic and almost farcical scene he planned to claim sanctuary inside the Bishop's palace. George's final desperate act came after accidentally leaving the £800 pounds he had borrowed to pay his debts inside a hansom cab. He then took his own life because he believed the money was irrecoverable. It can have been little consolation to the Glasse family to read that most of it had now been found by investigators who had followed up on reports of a London cab driver having come into money.[236]

In 1815, John and Anna Maria Glasse moved from the hall overlooking the church to a house diagonally opposite 'in the wide part of the street'.[237] Their new home was Burnham House, a seventeenth-century building which had just been modernised with a fashionable Georgian façade. It was also where Anna Maria and Roger Martin spent most of their childhood years and later became Bernard Gilpin's rectory.[238]

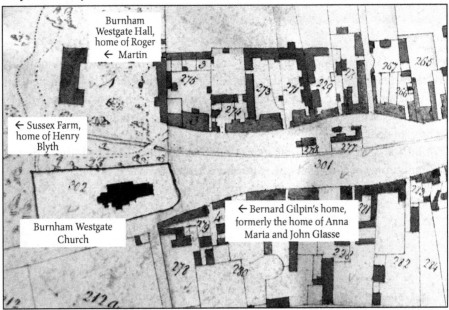

An extract from the Burnham Westgate tithe map of 1837[239]

The following spring saw 16 year old Horatia Nelson come to live next door to John and Anna Maria Glasse. She moved in with the family of Admiral Nelson's deceased sister Susannah Bolton. A bond formed between John Glasse and Horatia. When the rector prepared Horatia for her confirmation he gave her a book she treasured for the rest of her life. In it was inscribed 'Horatia Nelson, from her very sincere friend John Glasse, Burnham March 16th 1817'.[240]

Despite his wife's large inheritance under her father's will John Glasse was in financial trouble by 1818. In September of that year he made an unsuccessful

Burnham Westgate circa 1911

attempt to borrow £1,000 from West Norfolk landowner Anthony Hammond of Westacre despite not knowing him personally.[241] In his begging letter John went on to say that he felt 'a pecuniary transaction was managed with the least awkwardness between persons who are not in the habits of intimacy which commonly excite feelings of delicacy on both sides'.[242]

John Glasse explained in his letter that his need for a loan had arisen due to the bankruptcy of a Mr Dawson, with whom he had invested £400 of trust money. He had, he said, 'suffered him to appropriate this money to his own use, giving me

The village circa 1919

his bond for it, and by virtue of which I shall now only receive a few shillings in the pound in common with other creditors'.[243] To replace the £400 and for other purposes John Glasse asked Anthony Hammond if he would immediately lend him £1000 so he could replace the £400 and for other purposes. In return he offered whatever security was deemed satisfactory. He went on:

> Probably you may not think any bond sufficient security, if not, I can offer
> you a mortgage upon my property here, which is perfectly free from any
> incumbrance, and is worth about £3000. Mr. Stokes of Fakenham is my
> Solicitor, and I will enable him to answer any question you may wish to ask,
> provided you feel disposed to comply with my request.[244]

Anthony Hammond abruptly noted his surprise at the request in a draft response written on the back of John's letter. In it he wondered why John had applied to him for money and not his banker, 'especially as money is now become much more plentiful'.[245] Within a couple of months of writing this letter it looked as if at least some of what John Glasse was owed would be alleviated. Advertisements appeared in newspapers announcing the sales of properties in Norfolk belonging to the bankrupt bookseller and printer John Dawson of Foulsham in order to pay his debts. One of these was in Burnham Westgate and one of the people would-be purchasers could obtain details about it from was Reverend John Glasse.[246]

Time passed: In 1822, Horatia Nelson married John Glasse's curate Philip Ward. The couple moved in with John and Anna Maria at Burnham House and Horatia gave birth to her first child there. By the summer of 1823 Philip Ward had been offered the living at Stanhoe and the couple left Burnham Westgate for good.[247]

John Glasse had more money problems in 1824. He approached the trustees of Horatia Nelson's inheritance for a loan as he was in 'want of 1600 on mortgage',[248] but there is no evidence that this loan was ever arranged. The letter relating to this loan is one of the few specific source citations provided by Horatia's biographer Winifred Gérin with regards to John Glasse and the Martin family.[249]

The unfortunate cleric was subjected to other pressures during the 1820s when he became embroiled in a legal dispute between relatives. John's mother had died and his father, Reverend John Glasse senior, had married a wealthy widow called Susannah Charlton. The new Mrs Glasse had two sons of her own — Edmund and Francis Charlton. Court proceedings began between Edmund Charlton and his stepfather over Susannah's annuity whilst she was still alive and continued after her death. The four men all ended up in court over Edmund's attempt to mortgage his mother's estates in Shropshire to pay off a debt of £26,000.[250]

The dispute dragged on for several years, although there was some degree of reconciliation between stepson and stepfather before John Glasse senior died on

Burnham
Sept 9th 1818

Sir

Though I have not the pleasure,
of being personally known to you,
yet my name, & something of
my Character may probably have
reached your Ears ___ Indeed it's
because I am not personally
known to you, that I now address
you, for I feel that a Pecuniary
transaction is managed with the
least awkwardness between persons
who are not in those habits of
intimacy which comonly excite
feelings of delicacy on both sides.

A person here (Mr Dawson)
in whom I placed confidence, has
suddenly become a Bankrupt &
I shall lose 400 by his failure ___
This 400 was Trust money

The 1818 letter to Anthony Hammond, including mention of Dawson's bankruptcy.

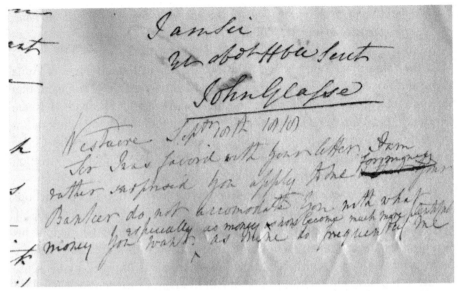

The note of refusal from Hammond, written on the end of Glasse's request.

the 13th January 1830 whilst visiting his son in Norfolk.[251] During a dinner held at his nephew Sir Roger Martin's house with ten relatives the 88 year old was 'seized by a slight degree of choking'.[252] Having walked into the adjoining room he immediately expired without any struggle, leaving those who knew him to mourn his venerable qualities.[253] John Glasse junior was appointed executor of his father's will and received gifts of silver and the remainder of his father's estate after all other bequests were paid. Despite this inheritance it became clear that financial worries were still not far from his mind.

'Next came the appalling news of Mr. Glasse's death, the result of an harassed mind'.[254] John Glasse 'had died by his own hand'[255] on the 13th September 1831, 'financially embarrassed'.[256] The dismay at the 59-year old committing suicide emerges in the reminiscences of Elizabeth Jones and letters written in 1831 and 1832 by his step-cousin, Reverend Henry Crowe, who lived nearby.[257] As the correspondents expressed pity for the widow of the unfortunate man,[258] John's financial problems and inefficiency as a trustee and executor for his father's estate and other duties were discussed.[259] Henry Crowe's first letter records how he hoped to get the late executor's accounts although he feared they were in disorder.[260] Commenting on the unfinished business Henry Crowe went on to say:

> That system of silence and secrecy which has characterised several of one family, seems to have extended to Mr. Forby and Mr. Glasse, the other two executors. They appeared to think me suspicious in my enquiries and gave

me but superficial information. Mr G I am afraid, dies embarrassed and I am
now prepared to find a ruffled skein in my hands.[261]

At the same time Henry Crowe went on to refer to the aloofness of Anna
Maria and Roger's sister Louisa. This was followed by the cryptic comment that
Sir Roger Martin 'is resolved to live and die a sportsman'.[262] Elizabeth Helsham
returned to Burnham Westgate to assist her grandmother in helping John's widow
'in making arrangements for giving up her house and accompanying Mrs. Glasse
to London'.[263] Anna Maria Glasse initially set up home at 30 Cambridge Street off
Edgeware Road, before moving to Slough.[264]

This tragic tale takes on more significance in relation to Roger Martin's actions
in the church five years later in another account of why John Glasse killed himself.
According to Horatia Nelson's biographer, Winifred Gérin, John Glasse took his
own life after Roger Martin refused to end his liaison with Mary Ann Clarke:[265]
Gérin paints a dramatic picture of how John Glasse was impelled by his sense
of duty as a pastor and relative to put an end to Roger's wrongdoing. He walked
across the green to visit his cousin at the hall on Tuesday 13th September to implore
him to give her up. But, Sir Roger did not care if his sins were exposed. Impervious
to his cousin's opinion he asked to be rid of his company.[266]

Gérin described how nothing John said could change his cousin's attitude. Sir
Roger was adamant that 'the lady was necessary to his pleasure'.[267] As such she
would remain in her post as his housekeeper. Gérin's account goes on to say that:

> Unaccustomed, perhaps, to dealing with colonial gentlemen, Mr. Glasse
> was at first incredulous, and then stricken to the soul with the failure of
> his mission; and realising how hurtful to his flock at Burnham Sir Roger's
> example would be, he took responsibility for it upon himself, walked home to
> Burnham House, and killed himself.[268]

There is no doubt that John Glasse was in a delicate position as a clergyman with
regards to his brother-in-law having an affair with his housekeeper. Frustratingly,
the only source given to support Gérin's highly charged version of events is a
vague mention of her having access to private papers.[269] Whilst the lack of citation
means that following up on this tale is a monumental task, Gérin was an acclaimed
biographer, most notably of the Brontës. One can only surmise that it was gleaned
from letters or diaries belonging to Horatia Nelson or her husband. Nevertheless,
Horatia could only have heard it second hand as she had moved away six years
before the tragic death of her former spiritual advisor.

Whilst it is a very specific and detailed description of how Roger Martin's
affair with Mary Ann Clarke caused John Glasse to kill himself there are some

inconsistencies. John's son, Bulkeley Glasse, remained extremely close to his uncle after his father's death. Bulkeley was the messenger mentioned in the 1836 handbills. He named his own son Roger, was in attendance at Sir Roger's deathbed and was a major beneficiary in his uncle's will.[270]

It is also difficult to credit the rector being so traumatised by Sir Roger's immoral behaviour that he would kill himself, even though they were related. After all other family members and friends had been involved in disturbing scandals; some of which were well known in the wider world. Whilst John Glasse could certainly not condone Roger and Mary Ann living together as man and wife when they were not, the question is whether it could really have driven him to take such a horrific step. Gérin's own account of how John and Anna Maria welcomed the illegitimate Horatia Nelson into their home tends to contradict this notion somewhat. After all she was the product of an equally irregular relationship.[271]

Despite the terrible sin of suicide, especially for an ordained clergyman, the acting incumbent allowed John Glasse to be buried in the churchyard. This may, as Gérin suggests, have been because of his 'long and faithful service and decent life'.[272] Suicide was officially a crime of *felo de se* (meaning a 'felon of himself' or 'self murder') until the 1960s. Those who survived an attempt could be imprisoned or sent to an asylum. A kinder finding would be if John Glasse had been 'seduced by the devil', as so many suicides were categorised, meaning he was not truly responsible for his own actions. This was a term commonly used by coroners until well into the mid-1800s. It was generally interpreted as meaning someone was not of sound mind and therefore not responsible for their own actions.[273]

Whilst there are many accounts of suicides being buried at crossroads, sometime with stakes driven through the heart, most were buried in churchyards. This was partly for practical reasons, as before the introduction of civil cemeteries in the mid-1800s there were few alternatives. The Church of England left it to the discretion of each incumbent, with such burials frequently taking place in the northern end of a churchyard, also reserved for nonconformists and those who died unbaptised.[274]

In the case of John Glasse there was no hiding away of his grave. The diocese granted approval for the vault and palisading around it. A stained glass memorial window to him and his wife can be seen inside the church. Interestingly, only the briefest of death notices appeared in newspapers and the only detail given was that John Glasse was a magistrate. Nor was there a coroner's inquest reported in local newspapers as was the norm for sudden, unexplained and violent deaths.[275] Whether this absence of public comment was an attempt to lessen the stigma and public embarrassment because John Glasse was a vicar and gentleman can never be known.

The overall impression is of a man beset by financial problems and weighed down by other responsibilities. He had been caught up in his father's legal dispute with his stepbrother right up to when his father died in 1830. Whether these law suits and other matters had an impact on John's overall state of mind can only be surmised. Perhaps he had further bad investments, or never fully recovered from his losses in 1818. He may, as implied by Henry Crowe, have not been very good at keeping accounts for the estates he was responsible for administering. Being an executor or a trustee may have been something John Glasse felt obligated to do whether or not he really wanted to as it was a task frequently undertaken by clerics. The snippets that survive from those who were there at the time indicate that such burdens did play a part.

Everilda Barnard had continued to visit Burnham Market until the death of her brother-in-law John Glasse in 1831.[276] Whether she continued to do so after her sister Anna Maria moved away seems unlikely. Everilda died in 1840, just four years after Roger behaved so provocatively in church. Her will made no mention of him or her surviving sisters. Her sister Caroline died eight years later, but some of the various cousins evidently remained in touch.[277]

9

A Very Questionable Character

On that summer's day in 1836 when Reverend Bernard Gilpin declared Mary Ann Clarke to have 'a very questionable character',[278] he revealed his strong sense of public duty. He believed that Roger Martin had the best interests of his country and the more immediate neighbourhood in particular at heart.[279] However, his position did not in Gilpin's view absolve Sir Roger from being taken to task for deliberately flouting the conventions of their age.[280]

What little is known of Sir Roger's companion, Mary Ann Clarke, indicates she was of a lower social status. Still, they were both single and there were no legal, financial or parental impediments. Having spent so long in India, where irregular relationships were common, it is possible to speculate Roger Martin had picked up 'unchristian' ideas. Certainly, the biographer of Horatia Nelson hints at this in a comment about Sir Roger and colonial gentlemen behaving differently.[281] She was of course referring to interracial relationships between white men and native women. These were known to have been commonplace, but were controversial for a number of reasons.

Many of these liaisons and the children born of them had an ambiguous legal status, even when acknowledged by the men. When Gérin linked Roger Martin's behaviour to his time in the colonies it was still widely believed that English men who had spent considerable time in India were likely to be corrupted and might not be able to act in a respectable manner once at home.

The attitude of men such as C Samuel Sneade Brown, a magistrate in India in the 1830s, reinforced deep prejudices over the pollution of white blood and fears that sexual subjugation by heathenish women was detrimental to British Christian values. At the end of the nineteenth century Sneade Brown published the letters he had written between 1828 and 1841. In one to his mother, he famously claimed that: 'those who have lived with a native woman for any length of time never marry a European; so amusingly playful, so anxious to oblige and please are they that a person after being accustomed to their society shrinks from the idea of encountering the whims or yielding to the fancies of an Englishwoman. I do not say the connection is a desirable one, but it should not be considered so heinous as persons in England are inclined to think it.'[282]

What is certain is that Ellen Clarke, the girl whom Roger Martin describes in his will as 'educating and bringing up'[283] was born around 1828.[284] At the same time he stated that Mary Ann Clarke had 'for some years past resided and now resides with me as a companion'.[285] Roger left Ellen over £1,500 outright and a yearly annuity of £100. Her special position within the household and his generosity is the strongest indication that she was his and Mary Ann Clarke's illegitimate daughter, although she is never described as such on any official documents.

In fact, Ellen was always presented as Mary Ann's niece.[286] She described her as such when she left her the bulk of her estate in her will. What is telling is that Mary Ann Clarke never mentions who Ellen's parents were, despite doing so for every other niece, nephew, great niece and great nephew she named in her will.[287] One interpretation for this is that she was reluctant to put a falsehood on a legal document which might affect Ellen's inheritance if uncovered.

Mary Ann Clarke remains a shadowy figure. The only time we hear her voice directly is in her will, written in 1885 at the age of 90.[288] Despite being at the centre of this scandal we get no sense of her thoughts or feelings, or even of what she looked like. She certainly had some form of education as she signed her will.[289] Our perceptions of her character rely on the words of four men; the three who were so vocal in that summer of 1836 and one of Roger's nephews.[290]

According to the biographer of Horatia Nelson it first came to the attention of Reverend Glasse that Sir Roger was having 'extra-marital relations' with his housekeeper in September 1831.[291] Exactly when and where they formed a relationship can only be guessed at, but it was likely to have been shortly after Sir Roger returned from India in 1828.

What has been uncovered is that Mary Ann Clarke was born on the 25th May 1795 and baptised on the 31st in Martham,[292] a small village in east Norfolk, around forty miles from Burnham Westgate.[293] Her parents, John and Sarah Clarke (née Cadge), married in 1791 in Sarah's home parish of Scottow, around thirty miles from the Burnhams. John was a farmer and Sarah came from a family of millers and flour dressers.[294] It is likely that Mary Ann was taught by her mother, or was sent to a local Dame school as when Sarah's father William Cadge died in 1780 he asked that the money from his estate should go towards his children's education and maintenance.[295]

John and Sarah Clarke settled in Martham, where they had several children.[296] Sarah was 'a woman possessed of many amiable qualities'.[297] She was only thirty-five when she died in February 1804 after a few hours illness, leaving 'a husband and seven children to bemoan their irreparable loss'.[298]

By the early 1830s, Mary Ann Clarke was living with Roger Martin at the hall. It is likely she became his housekeeper upon his return from India. Her younger brother George entered domestic service too, becoming butler to a family in Leamington Priors in Warwickshire.[299] Their brother William joined him there later, setting up as a coal merchant. Their other surviving brother Robert Claxton Clarke moved to Northwood in Hampshire where he married in 1830.[300] Mary Ann obviously retained close ties to George as she left bequests in her will to his children and grandchildren.

To all appearances Ellen Clarke was Mary Ann's niece. Ellen Clarke's age varies by up to a couple of years on different sources. Her birthplace was given as Scottow on most records, but her baptism did not take place there or in any of the seven Burnham parishes — the other place she was said to have been born.[301] Neither was Ellen Clarke baptised in Martham where Mary Ann Clarke was born.[302]

The village of Scottow is where Mary Ann's mother came from and her parents married. It is also where her brother John Cadge Clarke settled after his marriage.[303] It is five miles from the nearest market town of North Walsham. It only had 85 houses, 96 families and 434 people living there when the 1821 census was taken. By 1831 the numbers of houses and families had dropped slightly, but the total number of people living there had gone up to 460.[304]

On the 16th February 1833 a young girl called Ellen Clarke from Scottow was baptised two and a half miles away in the small village of Lammas with Little Hautbois. There was no compulsory birth registration at this time, but her birth date was written down in the margin of the register by the clerk conducting the service — probably because she was not a baby. Intriguingly, Ellen's birthday was given as the 17th August 1827 and her parents as John Cadge Clarke and his wife Elizabeth. Their residence was Scottow.[305]

John Cadge Clarke died in Scottow on the 23rd December 1828. His wife Elizabeth had predeceased him nearly two years before. She was buried in Scottow on the 2nd March 1827, aged 26 and a death notice was published two weeks later. No children are mentioned in either of their death notices.[306]

If Ellen was born in August of that year as stated on her baptism then she could not have been their child. The baptism took place nearly six years after the birth date provided and the clerk registering it was unlikely to question what he was told. This makes the omission of parents names in Mary Ann's will even more suggestive.[307] However, whilst this reinforces the likelihood that Ellen was really Mary Ann's daughter that date of birth means she could not have been Roger's as he was still in India.[308] That raises the possibility that she was really younger than stated on her baptism.

If, as it appears, Ellen was really Mary Ann Clarke's daughter her mother did something that thousands of women who had illegitimate children did: she created

The baptism register for Lammas, 1833.

a fictitious father for her child by using the name of a family member. If so, Ellen may never have known the truth, or simply not wanted to admit officially she was illegitimate.

The stigma surrounding an illegitimate birth is there for all to see in the frequent use of derogatory terms such as 'bastard' or 'base' on parish registers and other records in this period. It wasn't unknown for vicars to describe the mothers as whores, loose women, a man trap or similar as the incumbent of Middleton in Norfolk did in the early nineteenth century.[309] The notion of a cover up over Ellen Clarke's birth gains strength in the fact that the church preferred to welcome a child into the faith regardless of their parent's immorality. In Burnham Westgate for instance, between January 1813 and June 1841 there were a total of 634 baptisms. Out of these 46 were illegitimate children; just over seven per cent.[310]

No trace has been found of Ellen Clarke on the 1841 census returns. As such it is only possible to speculate as to whether she lived with relatives when she was an infant. When the census was taken for the night of the 6th June Mary Ann Clarke was listed as living at Burnham Westgate Hall and working as Sir Roger's housekeeper, but Ellen's name does not appear.[311] Neither was she listed with her Uncles George and William Clarke in Warwickshire, although she did spend time there later.[312]

It is not known what happened to Ellen's Uncle Robert after his marriage or whether her grandfather — Mary Ann's father — was still alive in 1841. The only other surviving sibling of Mary Ann's was her sister Ann, but there is no definite sighting of her on this census either. It is likely that Ann was in Norfolk at the time as her wedding to Thomas Watts of Buxton took place at St. Peter Mancroft church in Norwich in 1842.[313]

Ellen's absence may simply be because many census records for this period, including those for Scottow, are only partly legible. Moreover, the lack of birthplaces on this census and the practice of rounding the ages of those over fifteen down or up to the nearest five or zero means it is hard to identify those with a common name. Yet, Sir Roger's will which was written in April 1846 makes it clear that Ellen had been living at the hall for some time by then.[314] This raises the question as to whether she could really have been there when the census was taken five years before. The enumerators delivered the household forms to each residence for the head of households to fill in. They simply collected the completed forms afterwards unless the household head could not write or complete it for other reasons, or refused to do so. In that case the enumerator filled in the form themselves.

Despite Roger Martin's emphatic declaration in the handbills of 1836 that he had nothing to be ashamed of in his relationship with Mary Ann Clarke the couple did display some reticence on official documents. Mary Ann was described as Roger's housekeeper when the 1841 census was taken. Both she and Ellen were 'visiting' Roger Martin when the 1851 census was taken. They were unmarried and their occupations given as 'lady fund holders',[315] meaning they received some kind of annuity.

Five years later Ellen was living in Leamington Priors when she married John Overman of Burnham Sutton on the 11th September 1856. Her marriage certificate gives her father's name as John Cadge Clarke and an announcement in the local newspapers described her as: 'Ellen, only child of the late Mr. John Cadge Clarke, of Scottow, and adopted daughter of the late Sir R. Martin, of Burnham Westgate'.[316]

Sir Roger effectively admitted to having an affair with Mary Ann Clarke in the handbills. It was also clear from his statements on the matter that it was widely known of. He acknowledged that he had offended against the rules of society. In doing so he had submitted to the usual penalties imposed for such behaviour.[317] Sir Roger would however, 'not allow the indecent violence of a party to prevent me from occupying my seat in church as I may think fit, or from appearing in any other place where it is proper I should be present.'[318] He argued that apart from this one circumstance his conduct had been irreproachable. Yet Mr. Gilpin had disparaged his friend and companion who was Sir Roger said, 'as kind, as generous, and as truly virtuous, as any member of his own family.'[319] He went on to point out that he was equal to any of his neighbours in fulfilling his charitable obligations. But that which 'is more frequently administered by a female had been much impeded by unnecessary rudeness to Mrs Clarke while in the performance of her duty in that respect.'[320]

10

An imperative sense of duty

As a churchwarden, overseer and magistrate Henry Blyth knew Roger extremely well.[321] Before 1836, Roger Martin, Bernard Gilpin and Henry Blyth often attended the same official functions. When the Reform Bill had been passed in the summer of 1832, enabling greater numbers of men to vote in parliamentary elections, church bells rang across the county. Sir Roger and the Reverend presided at a meal for 1,100 poor villagers of Burnham Westgate and Burnham Sutton. There were great celebrations in Burnham Market with Sir Roger offering a bullock and his park for the occasion.[322]

Twenty tables were set up in the market place for inhabitants who were served roast beef, plum pudding and ale provided by subscriptions from the leading ladies and gentlemen of the two parishes. Sir Roger and Reverend Gilpin sat at the principal tables in front of an arch and a figure representing Britannia. At the other end of the rows of tables was another arch covered in evergreens and roses. The evening finished off with a pig race by the married men and foot races by the men and boys. A similar meal was generously provided the next day by Henry Blyth to a hundred poor from the parish of Burnham Deepdale.[323]

What happened in St. Mary's church in the summer of 1836 and the subsequent half-disguised challenge to a duel by Sir Roger can be set against the background of wider social changes. Elsewhere in Norfolk in the early part of 1836 there was news that a railway line was to be laid from London to Norwich, although it took nearly another fifty years before one reached the Burnhams. An Italian opera was performed at Norwich Theatre. Members of the new police force created by Peel went on duty for the first time in Norwich wearing a dark blue uniform with waterproof capes similar to those worn by the London police. Heavy gales swept across the county and one hundred and ninety five emigrants left villages close to King's Lynn to sail for a new life in Quebec.[324]

In 1835, just a year before the conflict between vicar, curate and baronet erupted, the trial and execution of two local women and a man for the murder of two adults, one baby and attempted murder of another man propelled Burnham Westgate into the national newspapers.[325] The tales of potions and spells at the centre of the Burnham Westgate case were believed wholeheartedly by many.[326]

The case put pressure on the income parish officials had to administer local affairs. Only two months before his quarrel with Roger Martin Henry Blyth had to apply to the courts for an extra £100 to defray the additional expenses incurred by the parish 'over and above what had been allowed'.[327] In doing so he described how the case, which involved adulterous affairs, a fortune teller and rumours of witchcraft 'was attended with considerable difficulty'.[328]

Although the witch hunting hysteria had passed its peak in England over a hundred years before, with the last execution for witchcraft in 1721, such beliefs were still prevalent, especially in rural areas. Historically, witchcraft accusations tended to take hold where there was strong economic, religious and social disharmony.

Murder, witchcraft and fortune telling, followed by the public wrangling between the vicar, his curate and the squire may represent a wider malaise in the village. Such frictions may go some way to explaining why Bernard Gilpin was so adamant in June 1836 that Sir Roger had an essential duty because of his position in society to set an example as the happiness of society mainly depended on peoples' moral character.[329]

A further clue to Henry Blyth's' reaction and feelings towards Roger Martin's actions that day in 1836 lies in his father's will. Henry Blyth senior died in 1831, shortly before Reverend John Glasse committed suicide. It is evident from Blyth's will, which he wrote in 1826, that he held John Glasse in high regard as he left him £25 as a memento'.[330]

Anna Maria Glasse moved to Slough.[331] She remained in touch with Lady Grenville, daughter of Lady Camelford. Elizabeth Jones wrote of how 'in my last visit to Mrs. Glasse at Slough she remarked that Lady Grenville had sent her gardeners from Dropmore to fill the beds of her little garden'.[332] After her death in 1853, her body was brought back to Burnham Westgate to be buried with her husband in the churchyard.

II

A foul hand

Roger Martin's act in ostentatiously seating Mary Ann Clarke in the family pew in June 1836 can easily be seen as a public statement by him in response to rumours over his brother-in-law's suicide. Not only did he declare that he had nothing to be ashamed of,[333] this dramatic act both physically and symbolically placed his mistress at the heart of his family. Sir Roger's call for satisfaction from the curate Henry Blythe for insulting Mary Ann undoubtedly came from his own sense of chivalry and nobility. Although it had been over thirty years since the Martins family friend Thomas Pitt had died in a duel, Sir Roger's own words and deeds reflected the same desire to defend a woman's reputation and his own against insults.

In his final written words on the dispute that erupted inside the church Roger Martin firmly stated his conviction it was proper for him to continue taking Mary Ann Clarke to church with him. Bernard Gilpin used his last published statement on the issue to vindicate his conduct. It was, he said, necessary to lay all that had passed between them before the parishioners in order to guard them against 'the influence of so dangerous an example'.[334]

On the 20th July 1836 Sir Roger declared that it was 'full time to put a stop to this state of things'.[335] The handbills offer no hint as to whether the three men ever resolved their differences. No report of this very public falling out between a lord of the manor, an esteemed clergyman and well-to-do farmer and curate appeared in any local newspaper at the time. Neither is it mentioned in any local histories.

All that remains is these three handwritten sheets of accusation and counter-accusation. They were stored amongst the papers of the Burnham Westgate Hall estate manager William Scholey. He worked for Sir Roger for many years, and continued managing the estate after Sir Roger's death. The handbills were later deposited at Norfolk Record Office by one of his descendants.[336] The other items in the Scholey collection were a pedigree of the Martin family, a newspaper cutting about a divorce case, a prospectus for a new form of agricultural accounts and a letter from William Scholey to his daughter Sophia.[337]

The broadsheets reveal that Sir Roger had already been ostracised. 'Female society', as he put it, including his nearest relations, refused to visit his house.[338] The confrontation in the church and the public pronouncements made by him, Reverend Gilpin and the curate Henry Blyth can hardly have gone unheeded by Sir Roger's peers.

Although the interchange between the three men makes it clear that Bernard Gilpin was unsuccessful in his attempt to make peace at the time, their lives were so intertwined with local parish, political and legal affairs they could hardly avoid each other. There is nothing to suggest Sir Roger became publicly isolated after June 1836 due to his relationship with Mary Ann.

Just three months after the fraught encounter in the church Sir Roger attended the Norwich music festival at St. Andrew's Hall for the benefit of the Norfolk and Norwich Hospital and an infirmary for the blind. This was a cause he had been involved with for several years, having previously served as Vice-President on the organising committee[339]

Sir Roger concentrated on running his estate and continuing his father's work in agricultural improvement. He had been involved in setting up the West Norfolk Agricultural Association. Two years before the confrontation in the church Mr Coke of Holkham Hall had toasted him at their annual dinner. The Burnhams were singled out in another speech as an example of how yields could be improved through judicious employment and firm treatment of the labouring classes. It is of interest to note that Anthony Hammond of Westacre, who John Glasse had unsuccessfully approached for a loan some years before, attended the same meeting.[340] One of Sir Roger's specialisms was cultivating opium, which he grew on a field opposite the rectory.[341] A mass of the opium collected by him was exhibited at the British Pharmaceutical Society conference in August 1868, where many members regarded it as the finest specimen they had seen.[342]

Sir Roger went on supporting political and philanthropic causes he felt strongly about. He also pursued an interest in natural history. A report appeared in newspapers in February 1837 of a 'destructive illumination of both Houses of Parliament'.[343] The reporter was called to witness a brilliant little star like ball diffusing a clear bluish light being used to illuminate the crypt of St. Stephen's Chapel.[344] This ball was the result of burning a mixture of hydrogen and oxygen gases.

Those worried about the potential for explosion recalled an anecdote concerning Sir Roger Martin. He was a keen amateur natural historian and had ordered a powerful microscope with a simple light bulb illuminated by this same mixture of gases.[345] Oxygen gas was pumped into a glass globe, probably with a pig's bladder. Hydrogen gas was then added through a jet and ignited. This would burn in the oxygen with a bluish white flame. The light could then be shone onto the mirror of the microscope allowing a brighter image than when using a candle. If the mix is not exactly right the whole apparatus will explode.

Sir Roger had a microscope constructed in London without regard to expense. Once brought to his country seat and put together there Sir Roger was highly pleased with its performance. However, after inspecting its construction and seeing the dangerous potential he had the artist repack it, made out 'his bill of disappointment on a liberal scale, and pack off, petard, microscope, fireball and all, by the next mail, for the metropolis'.[346]

In 1840, he was among more than 150 of the powerful gentry and clergy of the county in supporting the formation of an auxiliary society for the extinction of the slave trade and civilisation of Africa.[347] Just two years later he was one of the pall bearers at the funeral at Tittleshall church of Thomas William Coke, the Earl of Leicester.[348]

In the same decade Sir Roger was among the entrepreneurs and landowners who were actively concerned that Norfolk should benefit from the developing railway network. He seconded a proposal by Reverend Daniel Henry Lee Warner in 1844 that a direct railway from Wells to Thetford and London was required to 'sustain the agricultural interests of the county'.[349] It would, they argued, ensure the towns and villages the line passed through would gain 'the most important and substantial trading advantages'.[350] In February 1845 he became a trustee in a scheme to reclaim 30,000 acres of land for arable use from the sea at the Wash between King's Lynn and Lincolnshire. He, the Earl of Orford and the Duke of Portland were raising £300,000 capital by selling shares at £50 each.[351]

Reverend Bernard Gilpin died on the 26th December 1848 at the age of 76 after a long and painful illness. He had never married, but provided a home for one of his adult nephews for several years. During the seventeen years he served as rector he remained living in the house where Sir Roger and his sisters grew up opposite the entrance to the hall.[352]

In December 1854 Sir Roger's nephew and eldest godson Reverend Mordaunt Barnard was summoned to his death bed. Mordaunt Barnard was the eldest son of Roger's sister Everilda. He remained with Sir Roger as long as he could. Despite his uncle entreating him to stay Mordaunt had to leave before the end came having administered what spiritual assistance he could.[353]

Mordaunt Barnard's account of what happened next exposed much hatred and bitterness towards Mary Ann Clarke. After Sir Roger died on the 15th December Mordaunt was disinclined to attend the funeral. He was persuaded to go by his cousin Bulkeley Glasse and Mrs Clarke as they said Roger had wanted him to.[354] Mordaunt knew he had not been left a shilling, 'and therefore had no scruple in doing what was asked, arriving by the last train which would take me in time for the funeral and leaving Burnham by the first that would take me away'.[355] 'I would not', he said in a letter afterwards, 'remain her guest for an hour longer than the necessity of the case compelled me'.[356]

The letter in which Mordaunt Barnard described events to his cousin's half brother, Cecil Monro, a chief registrar at the Court of Chancery, only partially survives. In it he expressed his belief that Mary Ann Clarke and her solicitor had acted in a base manner to try and 'deflect the instruction of a dying man'.[357] Bulkeley Glasse told him of a memorandum Sir Roger had made in addition to his will. This was for Mary Ann to give £500 to Mordaunt Monro — Cecil's half brother and cousin to both Mordaunt and Bulkeley.

Mordaunt Barnard immediately feared that 'she would if possible defeat his intentions'.[358] He went on to describe how Kent, the solicitor, 'began to talk to me in what I plainly saw as a treacherous tone about Mrs C having every desire to fulfil R's intention, but as the gift was hers she feared that M M would not take it so, and evidently wishing to impress me with the opinion that he could not'.[359]

Mordaunt Barnard suspected a conspiracy between Mr Kent, the doctor Mr Dennis, who was one of the witnesses, and Mary Ann Clarke. This was to defeat Sir Roger's real intention by suggesting his mind had been wandering.[360] Augustine Valentine Dennis was an apothecary by training and coincidentally was at that time leasing Burnham House where Roger had grown up.

Mordaunt Barnard felt this devious plan 'ought to be an additional reason with M M to take the money.'[361] He went on to say he had written to Mr Kent asking him to offer his own prices for the family portraits, 'which I would rescue from such a foul hand if I could. Indeed I would almost give the money to have them burn'.[362] However, Mordaunt did not wish his name to appear in the matter of the £500 bequest as there had been no reply from Mrs Clarke as yet. He feared she would punish him for his intemperance with a refusal; 'tho' indeed she already well knows what I think'.[363]

There was more. Mordaunt Barnard questioned why the

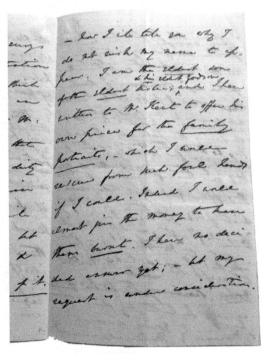

Part of the letter from Mordaunt Barnard.

witnesses to this document had not had it legalised by getting Sir Roger to make his mark as he had been doing on cheques until the very last. 'I believe', he said, that 'Mrs C (and I have ample reason for my bad opinion of her) to be capable of having intentionally omitted to do so, and of having contemplated at the very moment in which she received his dying injunction, how she might best defeat it'.[364]

Mordaunt Barnard was not done. He reiterated that Bulkeley Glass had made it clear what Sir Roger's wishes were. He expressly wanted this gift to Mordaunt Monro 'to be so binding on Mrs. Clarke that she would be driven to fulfil it… He clearly considered it as a thing which must be done, and could not be questioned.'[365]

There is no memorandum mentioning Mordaunt Monro appended to Sir Roger's will. In the will Sir Roger appointed Mary Ann Clarke sole executrix. He left her a yearly allowance and other generous bequests as long as she remained unmarried. It is striking that he used this clause — twice. It was typically only used with regards to wives. Making a bequest to a single woman contingent on such a restriction is virtually unknown as it was designed to prevent an inheritance from ending up in the hands of a new husband. This was because when Roger wrote his will married women had no automatic legal control over any property. If a widow remarried her property became her new husband's unless a marriage contract had been set up or the property put into trust in advance.

Mary Ann received all of Sir Roger's ready money, securities for money, household goods and personal estate

Sir Roger's will.

outright, as well as the use of his house and lands in trust until her death. This kept the Martin estate in the family with the hall and most of farm lands going to Sir Roger's nephew Bulkeley Glasse after Mary Ann's death.[366]

When it came to Ellen Clarke Sir Roger described her as his ward, 'whom I have educated and brought up and who now resides with me'.[367] He wrote his will in April 1846 and a codicil was added almost exactly six years later which trebled his bequests to Ellen. In total she received £1,500 outright and a £100 a year annuity, equivalent to nearly £90.000 and £6,000 a year in today's terms.[368]

12

Kind, generous & truly virtuous

After Roger Martin's death, Mary Ann Clarke continued living at Burnham Westgate Hall as the lady of the manor. Two years later, in 1856, Ellen married John Overman, a farmer from Burnham Overy, in Leamington Priors in Warwickshire. George Clarke, Mary Ann's brother, who worked as a butler there, was a witness.[369] In the marriage notice that appeared in the newspapers Ellen was described as 'the only child of the late Mr. John Clarke of Scottow and adopted daughter of the late Sir R. Martin'.[370]

Five years after Sir Roger died another Norfolk family became notorious because of the liaison between the heir to an estate and an unsuitable woman. When William Frederick Windham of Felbrigg Hall married a London courtesan in 1861 it resulted in a court case instigated by his uncle over William's mental capacity, abortive divorce proceedings, bankruptcy hearings and an ignominious death.[371]

Roger Martin had by some good fortune escaped his personal affairs being subjected to the same public scrutiny in the press and courts. Whilst rumours and hints about the illicit romance between him and Mary Ann have filtered out over the years from private papers the handbills obviously did not reach the attention of the news reporters. If they had it is hard to imagine they would have resisted recounting this tale of lord of a manor effectively challenging a curate to a duel over his lady friend. Whilst Roger's nephew Mordaunt Barnard was willing to complain about Mary Ann Clarke to his kinsman he never took any legal action. Perhaps he consulted a solicitor who told him there was no case. Or, he simply preferred to distance himself once and for all.

Life in Burnham Westgate continued much as before. Mary Ann's land agent William Scholey was innovative and sympathetic to the conditions of farm labourers. In 1864 he published a 'new and improved form of agricultural accounts' for noblemen, gentlemen's agents or stewards, which was dedicated to the president of the Provident and Members of the Docking Union Association'.[372]

Mary Ann's brother George died in Leamington Priors in August 1879. The same year Mary Ann's land agent William Scholey described to his daughter about how unsettled everything was due to agricultural strikes against wage reductions in Burnham and nearby Docking. The Burnham parishes were feeling the effects of the widespread agricultural depression that had begun in the early part of that decade. Cheap grain imports, poor harvests and outbreaks of cattle plague were among the contributory factors and rental incomes across the county dropped by up to half for landowners. The labourers at Thorpe had struck against a reduction in wages and masters had to give in he said, because the farmers would not agree to the reduction and 'the Docking farmers are locking out all the union men'.[373] Scholey felt 'it does away with the good feeling that ought to exist between master and man'.[374]

Mary Ann Clarke's continued presence at the hall and honorary title of 'lady of the manor' indicates she was eventually accepted at some level by locals.[375] The money left to them in Roger Martin's will ensured that she and Ellen Clarke were wealthy women which no doubt helped smooth over a certain amount of social awkwardness. Perhaps more importantly since that summer's day in 1836, many of the financial, social and legal obstacles facing women had lessened. Class boundaries were more blurred too as the rise of the middle classes, political reform and mass education contributed to a breakdown of the old order.

Mary Ann Clarke was branded as having a sinful, foul and a questionable character by clergymen and relatives. There is no doubting the revulsion some felt over their liaison. This has seeped down into modern accounts as evidenced by Gérin's biography of Horatia Nelson. Both Mary Ann Clarke and Lady Hamilton were perceived much more negatively than the men in their lives. Whilst the women tend to be presented as morally corrupt the men in their lives were more often characterised as weak or overwhelmed by emotions. The double standard for men and women over sexual affairs has remained alive and well.

Henry Etheridge Blyth died on the 21st December 1880 aged 82, and was buried in the same churchyard as Roger Martin.[376] No reports have been found in local newspapers that mention Mary Ann before Sir Roger's death. But she does appear from time to time in the decades afterwards. On Christmas Eve 1882 for instance she gave the poor widows of the parish their annual Christmas dinner and a quantity of coal.[377] Her position was undoubtedly made easier by the deaths of the two men who had called her character into question and objected so vociferously to her presence in the family pew all those years before. Yet the story passed down to Horatia Nelson's biographer reveals that some at least had long memories.

Mary Ann Clarke was still living at Burnham Westgate Hall at the time of her death on the 3rd January 1888 at the age of 92.[378] She was buried with Sir Roger Martin in a large tomb close to the churchyard wall adjoining the hall grounds. They are commemorated on the same gravestone, although no relationship between them is specified. She left over £20,000 in her will (worth between one and two million pounds today).[379]

Bulkeley Glasse sold his interest in the estate to Ellen and her husband John Overman. Ellen took over as lady of the manor, but only enjoyed her position for five years. Whether it was simply due to the passage of time, or the fact that John Overman came from a well established local farming family, but Ellen seems to have always been favourably received. Like Horatia Nelson before her, the perceived lack of moral character of their respective 'adoptive' mothers had not damaged her social standing. Even whilst Mary Ann Clarke was still alive Ellen and John both played an active part in parish affairs; organising festivities, school treats and attending social events. John Overman became a churchwarden at Burnham Westgate church. Before Henry Blyth's death the two men frequently attended meetings of the Burnham Westgate School Board, harvest festivals, agricultural shows and other celebrations and official groups alongside each other.[380]

When Ellen and John's son Robert Overman reached the age of twenty-one in 1880 they threw a party for the labourers who worked on their estate and their wives. Around seventy workers attended a dinner in a building in the grounds, with the catering supplied by the *Hoste Arms Hotel*. Whilst Mr Overman presided over the meal the ladies from the house assisted in waiting at table.[381] One can only wonder if one of them was the octogenarian Mary Ann Clarke.

Ellen Overman (née Clarke) died of paralysis, aged 66 on the 17th January 1893. She was buried in Burnham Westgate churchyard in a grave close to the one housing Roger Martin and Mary Ann Clarke.[382]

Back in 1836, Sir Roger Martin challenged the conventional social mores when he asserted that:

> In respect to taking Mrs. Clark to church with me, which is I conclude the matter to which you object, I can only say that on mature consideration I am perfectly convinced that under existing circumstances, it is proper that I should continue to do so.[383]

I like to think that he and Mary Ann Clarke continued going to church; sitting together in the family pew, with the Martin crest on the wall above their heads, the memorial to John and Anna Maria Glasse to one side, and within feet of the brass plated and marble monuments to Roger's parents and other relations. That, finally, others shared in Roger Martin's belief that Mary Ann Clarke was 'kind, generous and truly virtuous'.[384]

IN MEMORY OF SIR ROGER MARTIN BART
WHO DIED THE 15TH DEC^R. 1854
AGED 75 YEARS
ALSO OF
MARY ANN CLARKE
BORN MAY 25TH 1795
DIED JAN^Y. 3RD 1888

Gravestone of Roger Martin and Mary Ann Clarke

References

1 Handbills. 1836: In. Papers of the Scholey family of Burnham Westgate Hall, agents to Sir Roger Martin. NRO: MC 404/1-3, p.1.
2 Ibid., pp.1-3.
3 Pedigree. In: Papers of the Scholey family.Ibid. NRO: MC 404/4-5; Rye, Walter. 1913: *Norfolk Families*. Norwich, pp.536-537; Jones, Elizabeth. 1866: *Reminiscences of Elizabeth Jones (née Helsham), 1801-1866*. Caldwell-Heath Archive.
4 Handbills.Ibid, pp.1-3.
5 Ibid., p.1.
6 Ibid.
7 Ibid.
8 Gérin, Winifred. 1970: *Horatia Nelson*. Oxford University Press pp.258, 270, 291; Handbills. Ibid., p.1; Jones.Ibid.
9 Handbills.Ibid, p.1.
10 Ibid.
11 Ibid.
12 Ibid.
13 Ibid.
14 Ibid.
15 Ibid.
16 Ibid.
17 Ibid, pp.1-3.
18 Ibid., p.3.
19 Ibid.
20 Ibid, pp.1-3.
21 Ibid.
22 Ibid., p.3.
23 Ibid.
24 Ibid., p.2.
25 Ibid.
26 Ibid.
27 Ibid, p.3.
28 Brooks, Chris. 1995: *The Victorian Church: Architecture and Society*. Manchester University Press; Bennett, John Charles. [? post 2006]. *The English Anglican Practice of Pew-Renting, 1800-1960*. PhD Thesis, University of Birmingham, Chs. 4, 7 & 8.

29   Barnard, John and McKenzie, D. F. Eds. 2002: *The Cambridge History of the Book in Britain*. Cambridge University Press; Feather, John: 2006: *A History of British Publishing*. 2nd Edition. Routledge.

30   Bennett, Bridget, Ed. 1996: *Ripples of Dissent, Women's Stories of Marriage from the 1890s*. J.M. Dent & Sons; Waller, Maureen. 2009: *The English Marriage. Tales of Love, Money and Adultery*. John Murray.

31   Jones.Ibid; Gérin.Ibid., p.270.

32   Gérin,Ibid.

33   Ibid.

34   Waller.Ibid., pp.237-260.

35   Marriage notice, Ellen Clarke. In: *Bury and Norwich Post*, 24 Sept 1856; Will of Sir Roger Martin of Burnham Westgate, Norfolk, 1855. TNA: PROB/11/2205; Will of Mary Ann Clarke, spinster of Burnham Westgate, 1888.

36   Ibid.

37   Gérin.Ibid., p.270.

38   Bates, Dr., and Knowles Edward H. 1870 & 1951: *Historical Notes on Burnham Westgate*: In: Burnham Westgate Churchwardens Accounts, 1747-1861: NRO: PD 573/39-41; Martin Pedigree.Ibid; Rye;Ibid; 1841-1861 Census Returns; Norfolk Trade Directories, 1845-1900.

39   Bates and Knowles.Ibid; Obituaries and Death Notices. In: *Illustrated London News*, 30 Dec 1854; *Norfolk Chronicle*, 1854; *Carlisle Journal*, 5 Jan 1855; *Madras Almanac*. 1828-1830; *The Times*; Pedigree.Ibid. Rye.Ibid.

40   Bates and Knowles.Ibid; Kelly's Norfolk Directory, 1879; Cradle Hall Estate Survey and Map, 1796-1803. NRO: MC 1830/1; White, William. 1845 & 1854: *History, Gazetteer and Directory of Norfolk*.

41   Ibid; Newspapers [various]; Venn, J.A. 1900: *Alumni Cantabrigienses*, 1261-1900; White. 1845.Ibid. Blyth Wills [various]. NRO.

42   White. 1845.Ibid.

43   Venn.Ibid.

44   Handbills.Ibid., p.3.

45   Waller.Ibid., pp.237-260.

46   Handbills.Ibid., p.2.

47   Ibid., p.3.

48   Ibid., pp.2-3.

49   Jones.Ibid; Gérin.Ibid., pp.258, 270, 291.

50   Waller.Ibid., pp.237-260.

51   Handbills.Ibid., pp.1-3.

52   Ibid., p.1.

53   Hopton, Richard. 2008: *Pistols at Dawn. A History of Duelling*. Piatkus, pp.386-387.

54   Handbills.Ibid., p.1.

55   Ibid.

56   Hopton.Ibid., pp.1-5, 386-387; Jenkins, Bob. *The Last Duel in England*. In: *Portsmouth Now and Then*.

57   Tolstoy, Nikolai. 1978: *The Half-Mad Lord: Thomas Pitt, 2nd Baron Camelford (1775-1804)*. Jonathan Cape, pp.161-163.

58   Cradle Hall Estate Survey.Ibid.

59   Jones.Ibid.

60   Jones.Ibid; Dropmore Papers (Series II). Vol. CCLXXII. Letters to Lady Camelford and to her daughter Anne, Lady Grenville, of or relating to the Martin family; 1785-1802. © The British Library Board, Add MS 69309.

61   Tolstoy.Ibid., pp.161-163.

62   Ibid.

63   Hopton.Ibid., pp.4, 25-30, 44-45, 168-172; Jenkins.Ibid. Tolstoy.Ibid., pp.171-174, 180-186.

64   Hopton.Ibid; Jenkins.Ibid.

65   Burnham Westgate Parish Registers. NRO: PD 573/3.

66   Ibid.

67   Gérin.Ibid., pp.258, 270, 291; Handbills.Ibid., p.1; Jones.Ibid.

68   Jones.Ibid.

69   Jones.Ibid; Obituary of Sir Mordaunt Martin. *Norfolk Chronicle*, 30 Oct 1815.

70   Pedigree.Ibid; Rye.Ibid., pp.536-537; Jones.Ibid; Betham, Rev. William. 1802. *The Baronetage of England*. Volume 2. London. Newspapers (various).

71   Anna Maria Martin to Lady Camelford. 13 March 1801: In: Dropmore Papers.Ibid.

72   Burnham Westgate PRs.

73   Betham, Rev. William. 1802. *The Baronetage of England*. Volume 2. London.

74   Mordaunt Martin to Lady Camelford. 29 Dec 1793. Dropmore Papers.Ibid; *Stanstead Hall, Stanstead, Suffolk. Archaeological Evaluation Report*. Suffolk County Council. 2006: In: Archaeology Data Service; Will of Sir Mordaunt Martin of Burnham Westgate, Norfolk, 1816, TNA: PROB 11/1577.

75   Burnham Polsted Hall & Lexhams Manorial Court Books, 1756—1765. NRO: MC 1813/47; & 1769-1826. NRO: NRS pre-1955 Blomefield.

76   Letters from Martins. In: Dropmore Papers.Ibid; Matcham, Mary Eyre. 1911: *The Nelsons of Burnham Thorpe: A record of a Norfolk family compiled from unpublished letters and notebooks*. John Lane, London, p.106.

77   Letter Lady Elizabeth Foster to Lord Sheffield, 28 September 1793. East Sussex Record Office, AMS5440/217; Pedigree.Ibid.

78   Charterhouse School Records; Letter Horatio Nelson, 13 Oct 1792. In: Matcham.Ibid., p.92.

79   *The Illustrated London News*, 30 Dec 1854.

80   Jones.Ibid.

81   Ibid.

82   Anna Maria Martin to Lady Camelford. 1 Nov 1802. In: Dropmore Papers.Ibid.

83   Letters 1785-1802.Ibid.

84   Mordaunt Martin to Lady Camelford. 18 May 1782.Ibid.

85   Ibid.

86   Burnham Westgate PRs; Will of Reverend William Smith. NRO: ANF Will. William Smith, Burnham. 1766, fo. 182, no.7.

87   Defoe, Daniel. 1722: *Tour through the Eastern Counties of England, 1722*.

88   Population of Burnham Westgate. In: Overseers' Accounts, NRO: PD 288/1; White. 1845:Ibid.

89   Burnham Westgate Tithe Map, 1837. NRO: DN/TA 368; Manor Court Records.Ibid; Burnham House Title Deeds;Ibid.

90   Pedigree.Ibid; Rye.Ibid., pp.536-537; Jones.Ibid; Betham, Rev. William. 1802. *The Baronetage of England*. Volume 2. London. Newspapers (various).

91 Farming with Sainfoin. At: The Legume Plus Project; Obituary Sir Mordaunt Martin.Ibid; Letter Arthur Young of Bradfield Hall to the *Bury and Norwich Post*, 30 July 1817; Obituaries of Thomas William Cooke. In: *Bury and Norwich Post*, 27 July 1842 & *Norfolk Chronicle*, 2 July 1842; Articles In: *Norfolk Chronicle*, 10 Dec 1814; 2 Dec 1848; *Chester Chronicle*, 25 May 1813; 6 Nov 1858 et al; White. 1845 & 1854:Ibid.

92 Ibid.

93 English Heritage.

94 Swords, Barbara W. *Woman's Place in Jane Austen's England 1770-1820*. In: A Publication of the Jane Austen Society of North America. Persuasions 10, 1988, pp.76-82.

95 Gardiner, Everilda Anne. 1842: *Recollections of a Beloved Mother*. W. McDowall, London, pp.3-6.

96 Ibid.

97 Ibid., p.4.

98 Martin Letters 1785-1803.Ibid.

99 Mordaunt Martin to Camelford. 18 May 1782.Ibid.

100 Sophia Martin to Lady Camelford. 17 Jan [bef. 1784].Ibid.

101 Ibid.

102 Ibid.

103 Matcham.Ibid.

104 Letter Horatio Nelson. 13 Oct 1792. In: Matcham.Ibid., p. 92.

105 Mordaunt Martin to Lady Camelford. 30 Oct 1793:Ibid.

106 Mordaunt Martin to Lady Camelford. 29 Dec 1793.Ibid.

107 Ibid.

108 Edmund Nelson. In: Matcham,Ibid., p.105.

109 Nelson.Ibid; Currency Converter. The National Archives.

110 Martin Letters 1785-1803.Ibid.

111 Ibid.

112 *Ipswich Journal*. 20 Nov 1790.

113 Ketton-Cremer, R.W. 1948: *A Norfolk Gallery*. Faber and Faber, Ltd., pp. 216-217.

114 Mordaunt Martin to Lady Camelford. 6 Jan 1794:Ibid.

115 Ibid.

116 Ibid.

117 Ibid.

118 Ibid.

119 Ibid.

120 Ibid.

121 Ibid.

122 Ibid.

123 Everilda Martin to Lady Camelford. 2 June, Oct 1793, 24 Jan, 1 Sept 1794.Ibid; Letter Lady Elizabeth Foster. 28 Sept 1793.Ibid.

124 Lady Elizabeth Foster.Ibid.

125 Ibid.

126 Ibid.

127 Ibid.

128 Ibid.

129 Edmund Nelson. In: Matcham.Ibid., p.108.

130 Ibid., p.104.

131 Everilda Barnard (née Martin) to Lady Camelford. 24 Jan. [?1794].Ibid.

132 Notes on the Barnard family by Ashley Barnard, 2003. At: *Reminiscences of Elizabeth Jones* website.

133 Accounts, 1791, 1794, 1795. In: Dropmore Papers.Ibid.

134 Advertisement. 30th December 1790: Berrow's Worcester Journal.

135 Accounts.Ibid.

136 Horatio Nelson. 13 Oct 1792. In: Matcham.Ibid., p.92.

137 Edmund Nelson. In: Matcham.Ibid., p.108.

138 Accounts.Ibid.

139 Mordaunt Martin to Lady Camelford. 8 Jan 1795.Ibid.

140 T. Bradstock to Mordaunt Martin. 11 Aug 1795 In: Mordaunt Martin to Lady Camelford. 26 Nov 1795.Ibid.

141 Ibid.

142 Ibid.

143 Ibid.

144 Ibid.

145 T. Bradstock to Mordaunt Martin, 24 Aug 1795. In: Mordaunt Martin to Lady Camelford. 26 Nov 1795.Ibid.

146 Bradstock to Mordaunt Martin. 11 Aug 1795. In: Mordaunt Martin to Lady Camelford. 26 Nov 1795.Ibid.

147 Ibid.

148 Ibid.

149 Ibid.

150 Ibid.

151 Ibid.

152 Mordaunt Martin to T. Bradstock, 25 Aug 1795. In: Mordaunt Martin to Lady Camelford. 26 Nov 1795.Ibid.

153 T. Bradstock to Mordaunt Martin, 9 Nov 1795. In: Mordaunt Martin to Lady Camelford. 26 Nov 1795.Ibid.

154 Ibid.

155 Ibid.

156 Mordaunt Martin to Roger Martin. 12 Nov 1795. In: Mordaunt Martin to Lady Camelford. 26 Nov 1795.Ibid.

157 Obituaries of Sir Roger Martin. In: *Illustrated London News.* 30 Dec 1854: *Madras Almanac.* 1828-1830; Writers' Petition: Sir Roger Martin. 1795: BL: IOR: J/1/16/f.116.

158 Obituaries of Sir Roger Martin; *Madras Almanac;* Writers' Petition.Ibid.

159 Mordaunt Martin to George Matcham. In: Matcham.Ibid., p.168.

160 Ibid, pp.163-168.

161 Ibid., p.165.

162 Ibid., p.165.

163 Ibid., p.168.

164 Ibid., p.168.

165 Sophia Martin to Lady Camelford. 9 Nov 1800.Ibid.

166 Ibid.

167 Ibid.

168   Ibid.
169   Sophia Martin to Lady Camelford. [?Bef.1800].Ibid.
170   Anna Maria Martin to Lady Camelford, 11, 16, 18 Sept 1800.Ibid.
171   Burnham Westgate PRs; Death Notices of Lady Martin. In: *Ipswich Journal*, 27 Sept 1800, *Stamford Mercury*, 26 Sept 1800; Sophia Martin to Lady Camelford. 3 Oct 1800; Martin Monument in Burnham Westgate church.
172   Sophia Martin to Lady Camelford. 3 Oct 1800.Ibid.
173   Anna Maria Martin to Lady Camelford. 17 Sept 1801.Ibid.
174   Everilda Barnard to Lady Camelford. 15 April 1801.Ibid.
175   Ibid.
176   Everilda Barnard to Lady Camelford. 20 June 1801.Ibid.
177   Ibid.
178   Ibid.
179   Everilda Barnard to Lady Camelford. 21 Sept 1801.Ibid.
180   Ibid.
181   Ibid.
182   Ibid.
183   Ibid.
184   Ibid.
185   Ibid.
186   Anna Maria and Sophia Martin to Lady Camelford. 1800-1802.Ibid.
187   Sophia Martin to Lady Camelford. 1800-1802.Ibid.
188   Mordaunt Martin to Lady Camelford. 15 Aug 1801.Ibid
189   Ibid
190   Mordaunt Martin to Lady Camelford. 15 July 1802; Anna Maria Martin to Lady Camelford. 17 Sept 1801.
191   Everilda Barnard to Lady Camelford. 12 Dec 1801.Ibid.
192   Ibid.
193   Mordaunt Martin to Lady Camelford. 15 July 1802.Ibid
194   Anna Maria Martin to Lady Camelford. 17 June 1802.Ibid.
195   Ibid.
196   Ibid.
197   Anna Maria Martin to Lady Camelford. 25 Aug 1802.Ibid; Burnham Westgate PRs; Martin Monumental Inscription in Burnham Westgate Church; *Morning Post*, 17 Aug 1802.
198   Anna Maria Martin to Lady Camelford. 25 Aug 1802.Ibid.
199   Ibid.
200   John Glasse. In: Burnham Westgate PRs.Ibid. Matcham, p.105.Ibid.
201   Norfolk Marriage Index, 1801-1837; Ringstead Marriage Register; Marriage Notice. In: *Hampshire Chronicle*, 22 Aug 1808.
202   Jones.Ibid.
203   Ibid.
204   Burnham Westgate Manor Court Records.Ibid.
205   Handbills,Ibid.
206   Jones.Ibid.
207   Handbills.Ibid., pp.1-3
208   Jones.Ibid.

209 Ibid.

210 Notes on the Barnard family.Ibid.

211 Jones.Ibid.

212 Ibid.

213 Ibid.

214 Letters by Roger Martin in India. 1797-1807. BL Add MSS 37282; Letters to Wellesley, 1814-1815. BL IOR/H/643.

215 Jones.Ibid.

216 Obituary Sir Mordaunt Martin. *Norfolk Chronicle*, 1815; Burnham Westgate PRs.Ibid; Martin Monumental Inscription.Ibid.

217 *Bengal Directory*. 1815, 1822; *Original Calcutta Annual Directory and Calendar*. 1813; *Calcutta Annual Registry and Directory*. 1814; *Original Calcutta Annual Directory and Bengal Register*. 1817.

218 Jones.Ibid.

219 Ibid.

220 Mackie, Charles (ed.). 1901: *Norfolk Annals*, Vol. I, 1800-1850. Norwich; *Norfolk Chronicle* Newspaper, 27 Nov 1816; Burnham Westgate PRs.Ibid.

221 Jones.Ibid; Gérin.Ibid; Burnham Westgate Manor Court Records.Ibid.

222 Ibid.

223 *Bengal and Calcutta Directories and Registers*.Ibid.

224 Jones.Ibid.

225 Ibid.

226 Jones.Ibid; *Madras Almanac*. 1828-1830.Ibid.

227 Jones.Ibid.

228 Ibid.

229 Ibid.

230 Jones.Ibid; Marriage Notice of Everilda Martin and Thomas Barnard. In: *Kentish Weekly Post or Canterbury Journal*, 7 Jan 1794 & *Norfolk Chronicle*, 11 Jan 1794; Marriage Notice of Louisa Martin. In: *Ipswich Journal*, 17 Dec 1796; Death Notice of Frances Martin. In: *Bury & Norwich Post*, 11 Aug 1802 & *Morning Post*, 17 Aug 1802; Death Notice of Sophia Martin. In: *Morning Post*, 20 Nov 1827.

231 Letter to Cecil Monro from Mordaunt Barnard. 1854.Ibid; Letters Everilda Barnard to Lady Camelford. Dropmore Papers.Ibid; Jones.Ibid.

232 Gérin.Ibid., p.228; Letter to Anthony Hammond from John Glasse, 1818. NRO: Hammond of Westacre Collection, NRO: HMN 4/205; Letters from Henry Crowe to William Gunn. 30 Sept 1831, 28 Aug 1832. NRO: Archive of Revd. William Gunn. Volume IX. WGN 1/9/58, 1/9/72.

233 Jones.Ibid.

234 *Norfolk Chronicle and Norwich Gazette* 1811.

235 bid.

236 Ibid.

237 Jones.Ibid.

238 Burnham House Title Deeds; Gérin.Ibid., p.228.

239 Burnham Westgate Tithe Map, 1837: NRO: DN/TA 368.

240 Gérin.Ibid., p.228.

241 Will Sir Mordaunt Martin. 1816.Ibid; Letter to Anthony Hammond, 1818.Ibid.

242 Ibid.
243 Ibid.
244 Ibid.
245 Ibid.
246 *London Gazette*, 1 Dec 1818; *Norfolk Chronicle*, 7 Nov 1818.
247 Gérin.Ibid, pp.235-253.
248 Ibid., p.258.
249 Ibid., p.258.
250 Letters and draft answers between John Glasse, Mrs Glasse (formerly Mrs Charlton), Edmund and Francis Charlton her sons, and John Glasse, son of John Glasse, and G. Turbeville. In: Shropshire Archives. Ludford Park Collection. 11/905-983.
251 Ibid.
252 Death Notice. In *Bury and Norwich Post* Newspaper, 27 Jan 1830.
253 Ibid.
254 Jones.Ibid.
255 Letter Crowe, 28 Aug 1832.Ibid; *Norfolk Chronicle*, 27 Sept 1831.
256 Jones.Ibid; Letter Crowe, 28 Aug 1832.Ibid.
257 Jones.Ibid; Letters Crowe 30 Sept 1831, 28 Aug 1832.Ibid.
258 Letter Crowe, 28 Aug 1832.Ibid.
259 Ibid.
260 Ibid.
261 Letters Crowe. 30 Sept 1831, 28 Aug 1832.Ibid.
262 Ibid.
263 Jones.Ibid.
264 Burnham Westgate PRs; Jones.Ibid; Records of the Sun Fire Office. 16 March 1832: London Metropolitan Archives. MS 11936/533/1136854.
265 Gérin.Ibid, p.270.
266 Ibid, p.270.
267 Ibid., p.270.
268 Ibid., p.270.
269 Ibid., p.270.
270 Handbills.Ibid., p.2; Will of William Bulkeley Glasse, 1891; Will of Sir Roger Martin of Burnham Westgate, Norfolk, 1855. TNA: PROB/11/2205; Letter to Cecil Monro from Mordaunt Barnard. 1854: LMA: ACC/1063/254.
271 Gérin.Ibid., p.270.
272 Ibid., pp.228-229, 258, 270, 291.
273 Authors a priori knowledge and research, including transcribing Norwich City Coroners' records 1669-1835.
274 Author.Ibid.
275 *Norfolk Chronicle, Norwich Gazette* and *The Times* newspapers, Sept 1831-March 1832. British Newspaper Collection online. BL.
276 Jones.Ibid.
277 Will of Everilda Barnard, PCC 1840. TNA: PROB 11/1921; Death Notice of Everilda Barnard, 1840; Death Notice of Caroline Monro, 1848. In: *London Evening Standard*, 2 Jun 1848.
278 Handbills.Ibid., p.2.

279 Ibid., p.2.
280 Ibid., p.2.
281 Gérin.Ibid., p.270.
282 Sneade Brown, Samuel. 2011: *Home Letters Written from India: Between the Years 1828 and 1841*. Cambridge University Press, p.17.
283 Will Sir Roger Martin.Ibid.
284 Will.Ibid; 1851-1891 Census Returns.Ibid.
285 Will Roger Martin.Ibid.
286 Marriage Certificate, Ellen Clarke, 1854; Lammas with Buxton PRs; Marriage notice of Ellen Clarke. In: *Bury and Norwich Post*, 24 Sept 1856; Will of Mary Ann Clarke, spinster of Burnham Westgate, 1888.
287 Will Mary Ann Clarke, 1888.Ibid.
288 Ibid.
289 Ibid.
290 Handbills.Ibid., pp.1-3; Letter to Cecil Monro from Mordaunt Barnard.Ibid.
291 Gérin.Ibid., p.270.
292 Gravestone of Mary Anne Clarke in Burnham Westgate Churchyard; Martham Parish Registers. NRO: PD 710.
293 1851-1911 Census Returns; Gravestone.Ibid; Martham PRs.Ibid.
294 Scottow Parish Registers. NRO: PD 145/5.
295 Will of William Cadge of Scottow, miller, NCC 25 Watson.
296 Scottow PRs.Ibid; Martham Parish Registers.Ibid; Death Notice. 1804.Ibid.
297 Death Notice of Sarah Clarke. In: *Norfolk Chronicle*, 4 Feb 1804.
298 Death Notice.Ibid.
299 1841-1881 Census Returns.
300 1841-1911 Census Returns; FamilySearch.
301 1851-1891 Census Returns; Burnham Westgate PRs; Gravestone Ellen Overman (née Clarke).
302 Scottow PRs; All Burnham Parishes Baptismal Registers, 1825-1835; Martham PRs.Ibid.
303 Scottow PRs; Martham PRs.Ibid.
304 Census Data 1821-1911. At: GENUKI Norfolk Page: Scottow; White. 1845.
305 Lammas with Little Hautbois Baptisms. NRO: PD 170/4.
306 Death Notice, Elizabeth, wife of John Cadge Clarke. In: *Norfolk Chronicle*, 17 March 1827; Death Notice, John Cadge Clarke. 24 Dec 1828.Ibid.
307 Will Mary Ann Clarke, 1888.Ibid.
308 Jones.Ibid; *Madras Almanac*.Ibid.
309 Middleton Baptismal Registers. NRO: PD 640/5.
310 Burnham Westgate PRs.Ibid.
311 1841 Census.Ibid
312 1841-1851 Census Returns; Marriage Certificate, Ellen Clarke, 1856.
313 Ibid; Norwich St. Peter Mancroft PR. *Norfolk Chronicle*. 17 Sept 1842.
314 Will Sir Roger Martin.Ibid.
315 1841-1851 Census Returns.
316 Marriage notice. In: *Bury and Norwich Post*, 24 Sept 1856.
317 Handbills.Ibid., p.3.
318 Ibid.

319 Ibid.

320 Ibid.

321 Burnham Market Society. 2001: *A 21st Century Walk Around Burnham*.

322 *Bury & Norwich Post*. 27 June 1832.

323 *Norfolk Chronicle*. 7 July 1832.

324 Mackie, Charles (ed.). 1901: *Norfolk Annals*, Vol. I, 1800-1850. Norwich.

325 *Norfolk Chronicle* 1835-1836 [various]; Trade Directories.Ibid; Burnham Market Society. Ibid.

326 *Norfolk Chronicle*.Ibid.

327 *Norfolk Chronicle* 16 April 1836.

328 Ibid.

329 Handbills.Ibid., p.2.

330 Will of Henry Blyth, Esq. of Burnham, Norfolk. PCC Will, 6 Aug 1831. TNA: PROB 11/1788.

331 Gérin.Ibid., p.270; Jones.Ibid.

332 Ibid.

333 Handbills.Ibid., p.2.

334 Ibid.

335 Ibid.

336 Ibid., pp.1-3.

337 Papers of the Scholey family.Ibid.

338 Handbills.Ibid., pp.1-3.

339 *Bury & Norwich Post*: 11 Aug 1830, 14 Sept 1833, 14 & 21 Sept 1836.

340 *Bury & Norwich Post*, 15 July 1835.

341 Obituary Sir Mordaunt Martin. Ibid; White, William. 1845 & 1854. Burnham Market Society.Ibid; *Norfolk News*, 20 Aug 1868.

342 *Norfolk News*, 20 Aug 1868.

343 *Morning Post*. 17 Feb 1837.

344 Ibid.

345 Ibid.

346 Ibid.

347 *Bury & Norwich Post*, 18 Nov 1840; *Essex Standard*. 20 Nov 1840.

348 *Bury & Norwich Post*, 13 July 1842.

349 *Bury & Norwich Post*. 30 Oct 1844.

350 Ibid.

351 *Morning Chronicle*. 5 Feb 1845.

352 Will, Reverend Bernard Gilpin, Clerk of Burnham Westgate, Norfolk, 1852. TNA: PROB 11/2158; Burnham Westgate PRs; *Clerical Obituary*. In: *Brighton Gazette*, 4 Jan 1849; *London Evening Standard*, 29 Dec 1848; *Norfolk News*, 6 Jan 1849.

353 Letter to Cecil Monro from Mordaunt Barnard. 1854: LMA: ACC/1063/254.

354 Ibid.

355 Ibid.

356 Ibid.

357 Ibid.

358 Ibid.

359 Ibid.

360 Ibid.

361   Ibid.

362   Ibid.

363   Ibid.

364   Ibid.

365   Ibid.

366   Will Sir Roger Martin.Ibid.

367   Ibid.

368   Will.Ibid; Currency Converter.Ibid.

369   Marriage Certificate, Ellen Clarke, 1856.

370   *Bury & Norwich Post*, 24 Sept 1856.

371   Heaton, Trevor. 2012: *A Scandal at Felbrigg: The true story of the notorious Miss Willoughby and 'Mad' Windham*. Bosworth.

372   Papers of the Scholey family. Ibid.

373   Ibid.

374   Ibid.

375   Trade Directories.Ibid. Census Returns.Ibid.

376   Burnham Westgate PRs; Gravestone of Henry Etheridge Blyth; *The Ipswich Journal*, 28 Dec 1880.

377   *Thetford & Watton Times and People's Weekly Journal*, 30 Dec 1882.

378   *Ipswich Journal*, 9 Jan 1888; Gravestone; Will of Mary Ann Clarke.

379   Gravestone of Roger Martin and Mary Ann Clarke; *Ipswich Journal*, 9 Jan 1888. Burnham Westgate PRs; Will Mary Ann Clarke, 1888.Ibid.

380   *Thetford & Watton Times and People's Weekly Journal* [various dates].

381   *Thetford & Watton Times and People's Weekly Journal*, 25 Sept 1880.

382   GRO Death Indexes; Will Mary Ann Clarke.Ibid; Death Certificate, Ellen Overman (née Clarke), 1893.

383   Handbills.Ibid., p3.

384   Ibid.

Timeline

Date	Event
1740	Birth of Mordaunt Martin.
1742	Birth of Everilda Dorothea Smith.
1758	Birth of Horatio Nelson in Burnham Thorpe.
1765	Sir Mordaunt Martin and Everilda Dorothea Smith marry.
1767-1778	Nine children born to Sir Mordaunt and Lady Everilda Dorothea Martin.
1768	John Glasse senior and Susannah Smith marry.
1770	Birth of Anna Maria Martin.
1772	Birth of John Glasse junior in Pencombe in Herefordshire.
	Birth of Bernard Gilpin in Whitehaven in Cumberland.
1775-1780	The Martins employ Jane Arden as a governess.
1778	Birth of Roger Martin.
1791	John Clarke and Sarah Cadge, the parents of Mary Ann Clarke, marry in Scottow.
Circa 1791	Roger Martin is sent to Mr Bradstock's school in Birlingham, Worcestershire.
1793	Everilda Martin, daughter of Mordaunt and Everilda, marries Reverend Thomas Barnard.
1795	Roger Martin enters the East India Company's Civil Services.
	Birth of Mary Ann Clarke in Martham in Norfolk

Circa 1798   Birth of Henry Etheridge Blyth; later the Burnham Westgate curate.

1799   Death of Reverend Thomas Barnard, husband of Roger's sister Everilda.

1800   Death of Lady Everilda Dorothea Martin.

1801   Birth of Elizabeth Helsham.

1803   Death of Lady Ann Camelford, wife of Thomas Pitt.

1804   John Glasse junior becomes rector of Burnham Westgate.

Thomas Pitt, the 2nd Lord Camelford, is killed in a duel.

1805   Marriage of first cousins Anna Maria Martin and John Glasse junior.

Mordaunt Martin buys Burnham Westgate Hall.

Death of Lord Horatio Nelson.

1806   Birth of Bulkeley Glasse.

1808   Sir Mordaunt Martin marries again to Catherine North (née Styleman).

1809   Suicide of John Glasse's cousin, Reverend George Henry Glasse.

1811   Roger Martin appointed as judge and magistrate of the district of Goruckpore in India.

1812   Sir Mordaunt Martin purchases the lordship of Burnham Westgatge Manor.

1815   Battle of Waterloo and end of Napoleonic Wars.

Death of Sir Mordaunt Martin.

John and Anna Maria Glasse move from Burnham Westgate Hall to Burnham House.

1817   Horatia Nelson moves into the house next door to the Glasse family in Burnham Westgate.

1818   John Glasse junior experiences financial difficulties.

1819   Roger Martin appointed as second judge of the provincial courts of Moorshedabad.

1822   Horatia Nelson marries Philip Ward. They live with the Glasse family until the following year.

1824   John Glasse junior suffers further financial problems.

1827   Death of Elizabeth, wife of John Cadge Clarke.

1828   Sir Roger Martin retires and returns to England.

            Death of John Cadge Clarke, brother of Mary Ann.

1830   Death of Reverend John Glasse senior.

1831   Death of Reverend John Glasse junior.

1833   Baptism of Ellen Clarke in Lammas with Little Hautbois in Norfolk.

1835   Burnham Westgate murder trial.

July 1836   Confrontation between Sir Roger Martin, Henry Etheridge Blyth and Bernard Gilpin.

1848   Death of Reverend Bernard Gilpin.

1851   Mary Ann and Ellen Clarke listed as visiting Roger Martin when the census was taken.

1853   Death of Anna Maria Glasse née Martin in Slough in Buckinghamshire.

1854   Death of Sir Roger Martin leaving his estate in trust to his nephew William Bulkely Glasse and a life interest in Burnham Hall to Mary Ann Clarke.

1856   Ellen Clarke marries John Overman of Burnham Sutton in Leamington Priors in Warwickshire.

1863   Proposed railway line through Burnham Westgate.

1879   Agricultural strikes against wage reductions in Burnham and Docking.

1880   Death of Henry Etheridge Blyth.

1888   Death of Mary Ann Clarke at Burnham Westgate Hall.

1890   Death of John Overman.

1893   Death of Ellen Overman (née Clarke)

Transcripts of Handbills

Transcript of Handbills, 1836 (NRO: MC 404/1-3)

NB. This document is transcribed exactly as the original document is written, including spelling, capitalisation and punctuation (or lack of).

Page 1

Mr. H. Blyth of Sussex Farm was rude and impertinent to me after Church Service on Sunday last. He refuses to make an adequate apology, or to adjust the matter in the way which is customary between Gentlemen, I therefore Post him as a Coward.

July 5th 36th R. Martin

Sir Roger Martin, Bart.

On Sunday last Sir Roger Martin, Bart. appeared at his Parish Church, in Burnham Westgate, accompanied by a Female who has for some years borne a very questionable character for respectability.

The attempt to introduce this Person thus publickly in society excited the indignation of the congregation and most of them felt it as an insult.

At the conclusion of the service, as the congregation were leaving Church, Mr. Blyth in passing Sir Roger's pew (he being then alone) asked his permission to speak to him on the subject, and requested that he would refrain from appearing so again: Sir Roger immediately took offence and abruptly leaving Mr. Blyth, joined the crowd.

About 5. P.M. the same day Mr. Blyth received a message by a friend of Sir Roger Martin requesting an apology for what had passed or an immediate hostile meeting: Mr. Blyth being alone (after asking one question which Sir Roger's Friend declined to answer) refused to take any steps until he had seen a Gentleman who should wait upon Sir Roger's friend the following morning Mr. Blyth's friend accordingly waited upon Sir Roger's with a note to the effect that Mr. Blyth intended no personal offence to Sir Roger Martin, and admitted that he was wrong in speaking to him in the Church, but feeling the affront to have first been given to himself, and the ladies with him, a feeling general in the congregation, he declined to retract the expressions he had used: Sir Roger Martin's friend not satisfied with this, again demanded a further apology or an hostile meeting, which Mr. Blyth again refused.

About 6. P.M. on the following day (yesterday) Handbills were distributed by Sir Roger Martin bearing his name, in which he denounced Mr. Blyth as a Coward. Mr. Blyth places his character in the hands of his friends, satisfied that in noticing this gross breach of Decorum, and of the established Rules of Society, he was only performing the Duty of a Neighbour in Defence of those who having some regard for there own respectability feel the conduct of Sir Roger Martin a [?..] insult to themselves.

[? ?] 21st H. E. Blyth

Page 2

To The Parishioners of Burnham

It is with sincere regret that I make this further appeal to you, my Parishioners, but having failed in every attempt to remove what you, as well as myself, must feel to be a gross affront to the propriety hitherto observed in the House of God, I have no other mode of proving to you how deeply I lament the violation of all decency, and how sincerely I desire that the baleful example may in no instance And to infringe upon that moral rectitude so essential to the good order and happiness of Society.

With this view soley I lay before you the correspondence that has passed between Sir Roger Martin and myself on this most painful occurrence. Believe me with the utmost sincerity, your faithful servant and affectionate Minister Bernard Gilpin.

Burnham July 15th 36

Sir,

After the interview which I had last week with Mr. Bulkley Glasse, and which I regret was not attended with its desired object, I am induced to address you upon this most painful subject; and in doing so, I trust I do not exceede the bounds either of my station, age, or the duties I owe to my parishioners, and I hope no expression I may now use will be construded into intention. An imperative sense of duty alone induces me to undertake this most ungrateful task.

I am sure, Sir, I do not assume too much when I say that as a well wisher to the Country at large, and to your more immediate neighbourhood in particular, you cannot be indifferent to the moral character of its population on which the happiness of Society mainly depends. Neither can you fail to acknowledge how essential to that moral character are the influence and example of the higher classes. Permit me then, Sir, to address you as the most influential person in the parish committed to my charge upon an occurrence which I will venture to hope would never have existed had you reflected upon the consequences of your indiscretion.

To err is the stamp of frail mortality — to repair our error bears the impress of an ingenious mind.

Sincerely as I desire your truest happiness, I assume no right of remonstrance upon your own conduct, except when remonstrance becomes a duty I dare no compromise.

Permit me then to hope that the mistake of an unguarded moment will yield to the mature reflection the subject so imperiously demands. Suffer me also to intreat you for your own sake — for the sacred office I fill — suffer me to intreat you in the name of your Fellow Parishioners — and in the name of that God in whose temple we meet here — and at whose bar of judgement we shall meet hereafter — suffer me to intreat you not to cast an affront upon that sacred temple and the Almighty Presence to whom it is dedicated, by conduct that general consent disallows in the intercourse of worldly society.

Though I will not allow myself to doubt of your compliance with my request made as the Minister of that God whom we meet together to worship I shall be much gratified by a line of acquiescence before we thus meet on Sunday next, as it will remove a most painful suspense from my mind which has suffered more on this subject than I can describe to you.

To Sir R. Martin, Bart, I am, Sir, your faithful Servant. B. Gilpin.

Over.

Page 3

To The Parishioners of Burnham

I am averse to parading my opinions before you, and should not ever have published this paper, but having been publicly reproached by Mr. Gilpin in the unusual form of a printed handbill — and having been abused to my face from the pulpit in coarse and violent language by his Curate — it is the only course left me to pursue. If I have committed sin, that is between God and myself — no man has a right to publicly condemn me.

I have I admit offended against the rules of society established in this country, and have in consequence experienced the loss of female society in my house, even that of my nearest relations. I was aware that I subjected myself to this grievance, and to the rudeness of the vulgar: but while I admit this — while I submit to the usual penalties imposed by society — I will not allow the indecent violence of a party to prevent me from occupying my seat in Church as I may think fit, or from appearing in any other place where it is proper I should be present.

Except in the one circumstance above alluded to, my conduct has been I trust irreproachable, and my friend and companion whom Mr. Gilpin is pleased to disparage, is I am convinced as kind, as generous, and as truly virtuous, as any member of his own family, In charity, I have not been behind my neighbours, but the exercise of that charity, which in its details is more frequently administred by a female, has been much impeded by unnecessary rudeness to Mrs. Clark while in the performance of her duty in that respect.

I think it full time to put a stop to this state of things, so far as it is in my power, and therefore publish this statement for the information of those amongst whom Mr. Gilpin's address of the 15th inst. has been circulated.

July 20th 36. R Martin

Page 4
Reply
Sir
I have had the honour to receive your letter of this day and date, and in reply beg to assure you that that I am fully sensible of your kind intention in addressing me. In respect to taking Mrs. Clark to Church with me, which is I conclude the matter to which you object, I can only say that on mature consideration I am perfectly convinced that under existing circumstances, it is proper that I should continue to do so. I regret that I disagree with you on any matter of opinion, but in acting as I think right I mean not to offend.

I am, Sir, with great respect
Yours very faithfully R Martin

Sir
I sincerely regret that the Appeal which I have made to you, has proved ineffectual. But as you adhere to determination of bringing Mrs. Clark with you to church and placing her in your own family pew, a situation reserved by decency and propriety for the pride and ornament of domestic life — you must not be surprised that I publicly appeal to my Parishioners both in vindication of my own conduct, and to guard them from the influence of so dangerous an example, by laying before them all that has passed between us.

I am Sir your faithful servant B Gilpin
To Sir Roger Martin Bart

Sources & Bibliography

The majority of sources used are held at the British Library, London Metropolitan Archives, Norfolk Record Office, Norfolk Heritage Centre, The National Archives and Sussex Archives. Some material was accessed online via the commercial genealogical websites Ancestry, findmypast and The Genealogist, and via the British Library, Early English Books, googlebooks, Project Gutenberg and the Society of Genealogists. The Reminiscences of Elizabeth Jones, 1801-1866 are part of the private Heath-Caldwell archive owned by J.J. Caldwell-Heath.

Abbreviations

ANF	Archdeaconry of Norfolk
ANW	*Archdeaconry of Norwich*
fo.	Folio
BL	British Library
GRO	General Registry Office
LMA	London Metropolitan Archives
NCC	Norwich Consistory Court
NFHS	Norfolk Family History Society
NHC	Norfolk Heritage Centre
NRO	Norfolk Record Office
PCC	Prerogative Court of Canterbury
PPR	Principle Probate Registry
TNA	The National Archives

Manuscript and Printed Primary Records

Abstract of Title to the Cradle Hall Estate. NRO: MC 542/1.
Advertisement. 30th December 1790: Berrow's Worcester Journal. At: http://

freepages.genealogy.rootsweb.ancestry.com/~dutillieul/ZOtherPapers/
BWJDec301790.html

Bates, Dr., and Knowles Edward H. 1870 & 1951: *Historical Notes on Burnham
Westgate*: In Burnham Westgate Churchwardens', Accounts, 1747-1861: NRO:
PD 573/39-41.

Bengal Directory. 1815, 1822: British Library.

Burnham Deepdale, Burnham Norton, Burnham Overy, Burnham Sutton with
Ulph and Burnham Thorpe Baptismal Registers, 1825-1841. NRO PD

Burnham House Title Deeds (courtesy of Anne and Malcolm Bailey)

Burnham Westgate Overseers' Accounts. NRO: PD 288/1.

Burnham Westgate Parish Magazines. NRO: PD 573/70.

Burnham Westgate Parish Registers. NRO: PD 573/1-6.

Burnham Westgate Polstead Hall & Lexhams Manor Court Records, 1756-1921.
NRO: MC 1813/47-49 & NRS pre-1955 Blomefield.

Burnham Westgate Tithe Map, 1837. NRO: DN/TA 368

Calcutta Annual Register and Directory. 1814: British Library.

Census Returns, 1841-1911. TNA: HO 107 – RG 14.

Cradle Hall Estate Survey and Map, 1796-1803. NRO: MC 1830/1, 852X7.

Crockford's Clerical Directories, 1868-1932.

Death Certificate, Ellen Overman (née Clarke), 1893.

Dropmore Papers (SERIES II). Vol. CCLXXII. Letters to Lady Camelford and to
her daughter Anne, Lady Grenville, of or relating to the Martin family; 1785-
1802. The British Library Board, Add MS 69309.

East India Company's Civil Service Writers' Petition for Roger Martin, 1796. India
Office Records, British Library. IOR: J/1/16, f.110.

Electoral Registers: Burnham Westgate [various]. NRO: C/Sca 1.

Foster, Joseph. 1886: *Alumni Oxonienses, 1500-1886.*

Handbills, 1836: In: Papers of the Scholey family of Burnham Westgate Hall, agents
to Sir Roger Martin. NRO: MC 404/1-3.

Heath-Caldwell Family Archives. Courtesy of J.J. Caldwell-Heath.

Illustrated London News, 1854.

Norwich City Coroners Records, 1669-1835. Norfolk Record Office.

Jones, Elizabeth (née Helsham). 1801-1866: *Reminiscences.* www.jjhc.info/
joneselizabeth1866diary.htm.

Letter from William Scholey to his daughter Sophia. 4 March 1879: In: Papers of the
Scholey Family. MC 404/6. 714X1.

Letter of Lady Elizabeth Foster to Lord Sheffield. 28 September 1793: East Sussex
Record Office, AMS5440/217.

Letter to Anthony Hammond from John Glasse. 1818: NRO: Hammond of
Westacre Collection, NRO: HMN 4/205.

Letter to Cecil Monro from Mordaunt Barnard [incomplete] - cousin of Cecil's half-brother Mordaunt. 1854: LMA ACC/1063/254.

Letters and draft answers between John Glasse, Mrs Glasse (formerly Mrs Charlton), Edmund and Francis Charlton her sons, and John Glasse, son of John Glasse, and G. Turbeville. In: Shropshire Archives. Ludford Park Collection. 11/905-983.

Lammas with Little Hautbois Baptismal Register. NRO PD 170/4.

Letters from Henry Crowe. 1832: In: Archive of Revd. William Gunn. NRO: Volume IX. WGN 1/9/58 & 72.

Letters from Sir Roger Martin in India: 1798; 1814-1816: British Library IOR/H/643, 656.

Madras Almanac. 1828-1830: Transcript at Families in British India Society www.fibis.org.

Marriage Certificate, Ellen Clarke and John Overman, 1856.

Martham, Norfolk Parish Registers. NRO: PD 710/3-5.

National Gazetteer of Britain. 1868.

NCC Marriage Licence Bonds, 1791.

News cuttings collection (selective). Norfolk Heritage Centre.

Newspapers [various] via British Newspaper Collection online at British Library and Findmypast website.

Norfolk Chronicle & Norwich Gazette Newspaper [various dates].

Norfolk District Probate Registry Indexes.

Norfolk Marriage Index, 1801-1837. Norfolk Family History Society.

Norfolk Poll Books [various]. Norfolk Heritage Centre.

Norfolk Trade Directories, 1822-1937 [gaps]. NHC.

Original Calcutta Annual Directory and Bengal Register. 1817: British Library.

Original Calcutta Annual Directory and Calendar. 1813: British Library.

Oxford Dictionary of National Biography.

Papers of the Scholey family of Burnham Westgate Hall, agents to Sir Roger Martin. NRO: MC 404/1-6. 715X1.

Papers re trial, for the murder by poisoning of Mary Taylor, 1831-1836: NRO: PD 288/3.

Pedigree of Sir Roger Martin, Bt, of Long Melford. NRO: MC 404/4, 5. 715X1.

Pers. Comm. Various 2009-2010: Diana Mansell: Burnham Market local historian.

Printed circular letter of William Scholey to accompany prospectus of his New and Improved Form for Agricultural Accounts. 1864: In: Papers of the Scholey Family. MC 404/6. 714X1.

Records of the Sun Fire Office. Anna Maria Glasse, widow. 16 March 1832: London Metropolitan Archives. MS 11936/533/1136854.

Ringstead Norfolk Marriage Register, 1808. NRO PD 696/22.

Scottow Norfolk Parish Registers. NRO: PD 145/3-5.

Survey of Burnham manors, nd [? 1796]. NRO: MC 1830/1.

Venn, J.A. 1900: *Alumni Cantabrigienses*, 1261-1900.

Will of Alice Foley, Widow of Burnham Westgate, PCC 1840. TNA: PROB 11/1922

Will of Anna Maria Glasse, Widow of Slough, Buckinghamshire. PCC 1853. TNA: PROB 11/2177.

Will of Baron Thomas Camelford, PCC 1804. TNA: PROB 11/1412/202.

Will of Baroness Ann Camelford, PCC 1803. TNA: PROB 11/1392/173.

Will of Elizabeth Smith of Burnham, 1780. ANF W62 f206.

Will of Everilda Dorothea Barnard, PCC 1840. TNA: PROB 11/1921.

Will of Henry Blyth, Esquire of Burnham, Norfolk, PCC 1831. TNA: PROB 11/1788.

Will of Henry Foley of Brancaster, 1824. NRO: ANF W91 f187

Will of John Cadge, flour dresser, Scottow, 1803, NCC 50 Barker.

Will of John Clarke, Gentleman of Leamington Priors, Warwickshire, PCC 1855. TNA: PROB 11/2209.

Will of John Overman of Burnham Sutton, 1888.

Will of Mary Ann Clarke, spinster of Burnham Westgate, 1888. PPR.

Will of Pinckney Wilkinson, PCC 1784. TNA: PROB 11/1115.

Will of Rev. John Glasse, Rector of Herefordshire, PCC 1830. TNA: PROB 11/1771.

Will of Reverend Bernard Gilpin, Clerk of Burnham Westgate, Norfolk, 1852. PCC Will TNA: PROB 11/2158.

Will of Reverend Bernard Gilpin, clerk, Burnham Westgate, 1849, NCC 193 Womack.

Will of Reverend Edward Gwynn Blyth, Clerk of Burnham Deepdale, Norfolk, PCC 1855. TNA: PROB 11/2205

Will of Reverend John Glasse, Rector of Burnham Westgate, Norfolk, PCC 1831. TNA: PROB 11/1793.

Will of Sarah Clarke, Widow of Leamington, Warwickshire, PCC 1850. TNA: PROB 11/2121.

Will of Sir Mordaunt Martin of Burnham Westgate, Norfolk, PCC 1816. TNA: PROB 11/1577.

Will of Sir Roger Martin of Burnham Westgate, Norfolk. PCC 1855. TNA: PROB 11/2205.

Will of Susanna Glasse, PCC 1831. TNA: PROB 11/1785.

Will of William Bulkley Glasse, 1891.

Will of William Cadge, miller, Scottow, 1782, NCC 25 Watson.

Will of William Smith of Burnham, 1766, ANF W7 fo. 182.

Will of William Smith of Burnham, 1801. ANF fo. 425, no 41.

Bibliography

Barnard, John and McKenzie, D.F. 2002: *The Cambridge History of the Book in Britain. Vols. IV-VI.* Cambridge University Press.

Bennett, Bridget, Ed. 1996: *Ripples of Dissent, Women's Stories of Marriage from the 1890s.* J.M. Dent & Sons.

Bennett, John Charles. [? post 2006]. *The English Anglican Practice of Pew-Renting, 1800-1960.* PhD Thesis, University of Birmingham. At: e-theses repository: http://etheses.bham.ac.uk/2864/1/Bennett_11_PhD.pdf

Betham, Rev. William. 1802. *The Baronetage of England.* Volume 2. London.

Blomefield, Francis. 1805: *An essay towards a topographical history of the County of Norfolk.* Charles Parkin (ed.). Norwich: William Miller.

Brooks, Chris. 1995: *The Victorian Church: Architecture and Society.* Manchester University Press.

Burnham Market Society. 2001: *A 21st Century Walk Around Burnham.* Burnham Market Society.

Defoe, Daniel. *Tour through the Eastern Counties of England, 1722.* At: Googlebooks.

Farming with Sainfoin. At: The Legume Plus Project. http://legumeplus.eu/farming-sainfoin.

Feather, John. 2006: *A History of British Publishing.* 2nd Edition. Routledge.

Gardiner, Everilda Anne. 1842: *Recollections of a Beloved Mother.* W. McDowall, London. At: https://archive.org/stream/recollectionsaboogardgoog#page/n15/mode/2up/search/Martin.

Gérin, Winifred. 1970: *Horatia Nelson.* Oxford University Press.

Goldman, Lawrence (ed.). 2007 *The Dictionary of National Biography.* Oxford University Press.

Heaton, Trevor. 2012: *A Scandal at Felbrigg: The true story of the notorious Miss Willoughby and 'Mad' Windham.* Bosworth.

Hibbard, Henry, M.A. 1937: *A History of Burnham Thorpe. Lord Nelson's Birthplace.* Rev. C.J. Isaacson. Norfolk: The Burnhams Rectory.

Hopton, Richard. *Pistols at Dawn.* 2008: *A History of Duelling.* Piatkus.

Jenkins, Bob (undated). *The Last Duel in England.* In *Portsmouth Now and Then* http://nowportsmouth.co.uk/galleries-and-articles-01/gallery-lastduel-01.html.

Ketton-Cremer, R.W. 1948: *A Norfolk Gallery.* Faber and Faber, Ltd.

Mackie, Charles, Ed. 1901: *Norfolk Annals, Vols. I & II'. 1800-1900.* Norwich.

Matcham, Mary Eyre. 1911: *The Nelsons of Burnham Thorpe: A record of a Norfolk family compiled from unpublished letters and notebooks, 1787-1842.* John Lane, London. At: www.archive.org/stream/nelsonsofburnhamoomatcuoft#page/176/mode/2up.

Norwich, John Julius. 1991: *A Country Parson: James Woodforde's Diary 1759-1802.*

Tiger Books International.

Pocock, Tom. 1995: *Norfolk*. Pimlico County History Guides.

Rye, Walter. 1885: *Pimlico County Histories. A History of Norfolk*. London: Pimlico.

Rye, Walter. 1913: *Norfolk Families*. Norwich.

Stanstead Hall, Stanstead, Suffolk. Archaeological Evaluation Report. Suffolk County Council. 2006: In: Archaeology Data Service: http:// archaeologydataservice.ac.uk/archiveDS/archiveDownload?t=arch-415-1/ dissemination/pdf/suffolkc1-15183_1.pdf.

Swords, Barbara W. *Woman's Place in Jane Austen's England 1770-1820*. In: A Publication of the Jane Austen Society of North America. Persuasions 10, 1988, pp.76-82.

The Gentleman's Magazine. 1855. Volumes 197-198.

Tolstoy, Nikolai. 1978: *The Half-Mad Lord. Thomas Pitt, 2nd Baron Camelford (1775-1804)*. Jonathan Cape.

Waller, Maureen. 2009: *The English Marriage. Tales of Love, Money and Adultery*. John Murray.

Websites

Ancestry.

British History Online.

British Newspaper Collection. At: Findmypast and the British Library.

Central England temperatures: monthly means 1659-1973: www.rmets.org/sites/ default/files/qj74manley.pdf

Currency Converter at: www.nationalarchives.gov.uk/currency/results.asp#mid

English Heritage.

Families in British India Society (FIBIS) www.fibis.org.

FamilySearch www.familysearch.org

Findmypast www.findmypast.co.uk

GENUKI: Norfolk www.origins.org.uk/genuki/NFK.

Historical Directories www.historicaldirectories.org.

London Gazette www.london-gazette.co.uk.

Norfolk Heritage Explorer www.heritage.norfolk.gov.uk.

Norfolk Sources www.norfolksources.gov.uk.

The Genealogist www.thegenealogist.co.uk.

The London Gazette www.thegazette.co.uk.

The National Archives.

The Times Digital Archive, 1785-1985.

Victoria County Histories.

Index